新东方
XDF.CN

MW01708287

Master IELTS 1

IELTS VOCABULARY FOCUS

IELTS核心词汇

编著/Jocelyn Lu

西安交通大学出版社
XI'AN JIAOTONG UNIVERSITY PRESS

图书在版编目(CIP)数据

IELTS核心词汇 / 陆文玲编著. —2版. —西安：西安交通大学出版社，2012（2019.9重印）
ISBN 978-7-5605-4422-9

Ⅰ. ①I… Ⅱ. ①陆… Ⅲ. ①IELTS—词汇—自学参考资料 Ⅳ. ①H313

中国版本图书馆CIP数据核字（2012）第123714号

陕版出图字：25—2008—033号

书　　名	IELTS核心词汇
编 著 者	陆文玲
责任编辑	孙冠群
封面设计	大愚设计
出版发行	西安交通大学出版社
地　　址	西安市兴庆南路10号（邮编：710049）
电　　话	（010）62605588（发行部）
	（029）82668315（总编室）
读者信箱	dywh@xdf.cn
印　　刷	涿州汇美亿浓印刷有限公司
字　　数	250千
开　　本	787mm×1092mm　1/16
印　　张	17
版　　次	2019年9月第1版第11次印刷
书　　号	ISBN 978-7-5605-4422-9/H·1396
定　　价	38.00元

CONTENTS

Master IELTS 1

IELTS VOCABULARY FOCUS 核心词汇

IELTS 常考主题必备词汇

IELTS 写作高分重点词汇

前　言

具备大量词汇并且懂得活用单词，是提升英语实力的不二法门。IELTS 考试中所出现的单词，没有冷僻、艰深或晦涩难懂的。不论是学术类(Academic)还是培训类(General Training)考试所出现的词汇，都在学习、生活、社会及基本常识等范畴之内。本书旨在让考生学习英语的同时，能够快速熟悉和掌握 IELTS 考试单词。

编者从过去多年的 IELTS 考题及十余本国内外 IELTS 权威参考书中，精心挑选出 IELTS 重要单词（第二版顺应考题趋势，增加了 200 个单词），分为 15 项主题，并依单词在 IELTS 考试中出现频率的高低分为高频、精选以及挑战单词三大类，在 IELTS 主考官的协助下编写此书，同时由多位 ESL 和 IELTS 外籍教师合作为单词造句并编写范文，希望让考生能够真正深入认识和灵活运用 IELTS 考试词汇，不再浪费时间死记硬背。

本书结构与特色

■ 根据 IELTS 考试所统计各主题词汇的出现频率，分成三大类：

☑☑☑ 高频单词：出现频率最高的单词。

☑☑□ 精选单词：经常出现且非常实用的单词。

☑□□ 挑战单词：较少出现的单词（通常出现在阅读中），难度较高，是取得高分（7 分以上）的关键。

■ 15 项主题式分类和写作必备用语：通过主题式分类，以有效且符合逻辑的方式记忆单词，增强学习速度与效果。

■ 标准英式词汇学习 MP3：聆听标准英式朗读词汇 MP3，以“声音记忆法”认识并记忆单词(即通过反复聆听 MP3 来熟悉单词的发音，进而自然记忆单词)。

■ 音标与中文释义：本书采用英式音标，聆听此书的 MP3，可以很快地进入英式英语的世界。由于大多数的单词在不同的上下文中有不同的定义，有些单词甚至同时有两个以上词性，因此在中文释义部分特别用“粗体字”标示出例句中所使用的定义和词性。

■ 新增同义词与派生词：为帮助考生更能活用 IELTS 词汇，特新增部分词汇的同义词、派生词、搭配等，各种标示及其代表的意义如下：

同 → 同义词　派 → 派生词　搭 → 词组与搭配　参 → 参考词汇

本书使用说明

练习前准备

■ 建议使用英式英英词典(不建议使用电子词典)。
■ 仔细阅读目录中的章节主题。
■ 一次(一天)学习一个章节主题。
■ 准备一张白纸，在白纸上先写下将要练习的主题。

练习步骤

1. 合上书，专心听 MP3。听第一次，不要中断。
2. 听第二次，将你认为你会的单词写在白纸上。
3. 打开书本，核对你写在白纸上的单词。
4. 先检查拼写是否正确，并看看书中的中文释义是否与你所了解的意思相同，然后看该单词的例句。
5. 对照书本，再听一次 MP3，圈出你不认识或不太熟悉的单词，仔细看中文释义及例句，并重复听该单词的 MP3 发音。
6. 合上书本，再听一次 MP3，把每一个你听出来的单词重新写在白纸上，同时写上其中文释义。对于仍不了解的单词，一定要查词典，找出更多的例句，加深你对该单词的认识。

注意事项

■ 每隔三到四天，再持续听已练习主题的 MP3。
■ 不熟悉的单词，一定要查词典了解其用法，最好同时找出同义词互相对照。
■ 随时播放 MP3，加强“声音记忆法”的效果。

英式音标・KK 音标对照表

元音	
英式音标	KK 音标
[ɪ]	[ɪ]
[e]	[ɛ]
[æ]	[æ]
[ɒ]	[ɑ], [ɔ]
[ʌ]	[ʌ]
[ʊ]	[ʊ]
[ə]	[ə], [ɚ]
[i]	[ɪ]
[u]	[ʊ]
[iː]	[i]
[ɑː]	[ɑ], [ɑr]
[ɔː]	[ɔ], [ɔr]
[uː]	[u]
[ɜː]	[ɝ]
[eɪ]	[e]
[aɪ]	[aɪ]
[ɔɪ]	[ɔɪ]
[əʊ]	[o]
[oʊ]	[o]
[aʊ]	[au]
[ɪə]	[ɪr]
[eə]	[ɛr]
[ʊə]	[ʊr]
[iə]	[jɚ]

辅音	
英式音标	KK 音标
[p]	[p]
[b]	[b]
[t]	[t]
[d]	[d]
[k]	[k]
[f]	[f]
[v]	[v]
[θ]	[θ]
[ð]	[ð]
[s]	[s]
[z]	[z]
[ʃ]	[ʃ]
[ʒ]	[ʒ]
[h]	[h]
[k]	[k]
[tʃ]	[tʃ]
[dʒ]	[dʒ]
[m]	[m]
[n]	[n]
[ŋ]	[ŋ]
[w]	[w]
[l]	[l]
[r]	[r]
[j]	[j]

About IELTS

IELTS（International English Language Testing System）“国际英语语言测试系统”是全球认可的英语语言能力评估系统，也是进入大多数英语系国家高等学府就读必备的英语能力证明，尤为英国、澳大利亚、新西兰、加拿大等国的教育系统所接受，而目前美国大多数大学也承认 IELTS 成绩。IELTS 测试分为“学术类”（Academic）与“培训类”（General Training），测试项目涵盖听、读、说、写，内容丰富、全面而多元，因此也可作一般性英语能力检测之用。除了计划前往英语系国家就读大学、研究生院、专科技术学院、预科课程者适合参加 IELTS 测试外，凡申请澳大利亚、新西兰、加拿大、美国移民者，或是担任英国及澳大利亚各政府部门实习生、参加国防部及公共医疗会议等的专业人士，都可以参加 IELTS 测试。IELTS 测试由英国文化协会（The British Council）、剑桥大学考试委员会 （Cambridge ESOL）及澳大利亚教育国际开发署（IDP Education Australia）共同举办，由 Cambridge ESOL 统筹管理。

IELTS 测试方式

IELTS 测试分为学术类（Academic）和培训类（General Training），测试内容分为听、读、说、写四部分，其中 Listening 和 Speaking 部分不分类，Reading 和 Writing 两项则分类。

■ 学术类（Academic）

主要用来评估考生在攻读本科或研究生等课程时，是否适合以英语作为学习的媒介。

■ 培训类（General Training）

适合前往英语系国家就读中学、工作或参与非学术单位培训计划的考生，许多国家也用以评估申请移民人士的英语程度。

IELTS 测试流程图

IELTS测试分为听力、阅读、写作、口语四部分，测试时间为2小时54分钟。

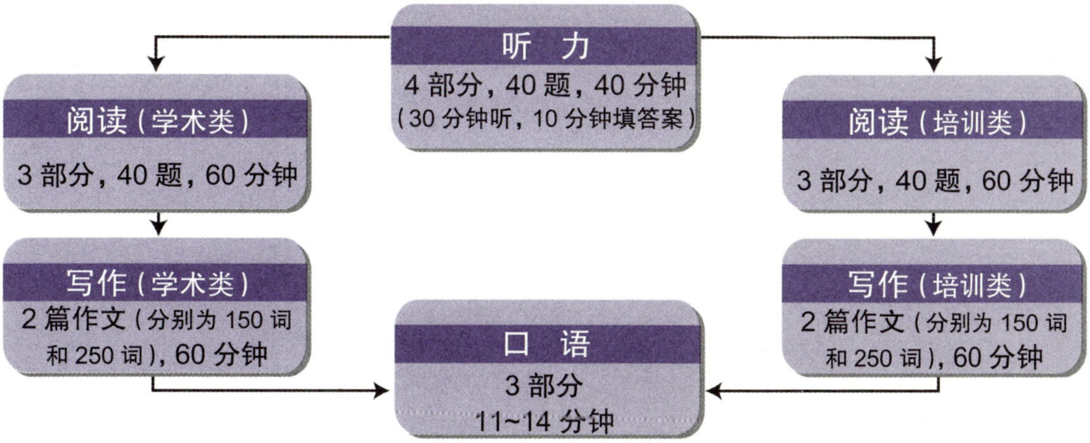

IELTS 测试内容

■ IELTS Listening Module·听力

内容	· 测试时间 40 分钟，其中 10 分钟填答案 · 分为 4 部分，共有 40 题 · 听力只放一遍，不会重复
题型结构	· 第一、二段：以一般生活及社会状态为主 · 第三、四段：涵盖教育、学术、世界性的主题 · 题型：选择题、填空题、简答题、图表题
作答重点	· 要边听边作答 · 需了解独白或对话的主题 · 注意数字、时间、日期等较明显的字眼 · 听出重要的词句，记下与主题相关或有因果关系的信息

■ IELTS Reading Module·阅读

内容	· 测试时间 1 小时，含填写答案时间 · 包含 3 篇文章，每篇约有 700～900 词 · 测试题目共 40 题
题型结构	· 主题多样化，除了日常生活，还包括学术上的探讨与了解 · 题型：简答题、选择题、匹配题、填空题、图表题、表格题、段落大意题、摘要题、是 / 非 / 未提及题（True/False/Not Given或Yes/No/Not Given）
作答重点	· 了解各段落主题与大意 · 圈出重要信息 · 圈出数字、日期、时间、项目等较明显的词句 · 不需要了解每一个单词的意思，不要浪费时间推敲不明白的地方

■ IELTS Writing Module·写作

内容	· 测试时间 1 小时，需写 2 篇作文 · Task 1：最少 150 词，建议花 20 分钟 · Task 2：最少 250 词，建议花 40 分钟
题型结构	· Task 1：考题基本形式为图片、表格、曲线图、饼状图等，考生依照所给的信息，分析、组织并讨论主题 · Task 2：依照所给的主题，表达自己的意见、支持或反驳、解决问题及讨论问题
作答重点	Task 1： · 避免使用自己没把握的单词和语法结构 · 从题目要求中，清楚分析题目，圈出重要的词或短语 Task 2： · 仔细阅读题目，避免文不对题 · 强调自己的想法和意见 · 支持或反对考题的论点，只能二选一，定位要清楚

■ IELTS Speaking Module·口试

内容	· 测试时间约11～14分钟，分成3个部分 Part 1：4～5分钟，自我介绍及面谈 Part 2：3～4分钟，1分钟准备，对特定话题发表看法 Part 3：4～5分钟，第二部分的延伸讨论，题目较第二部分抽象
题型结构	· Part 1：口试官介绍自己并确认考生身份，询问考生与个人有关的事物、家人、兴趣、工作背景等 · Part 2：口试官出示话题卡，考生依据话题卡可有1分钟的准备时间，考场备有纸笔供考生使用 · Part 3：连结第二部分的延伸讨论，或更深更广的互动讨论
作答重点	· 有效表达意见，与口试官沟通 · 正确使用词汇和语法 · 能够参与一般对话或勇于发问、发言 · 轻松应对，表达流畅，答为所问

IELTS 测试的一天

■ 笔试部分

时　间	考场建议
在早上8:00前 到达考场	· 请在考试当天上午8:00前到达考试中心。8:30以后停止进场。8:30以后到达考场的考生将被取消参加笔试的资格，并不得转考、退考或退费。笔试迟到的考生有权利选择参加口语考试。 · 在考场张贴的名单上找到自己的名字，记住自己的考场。 · 听从考试中心工作人员的指挥到候考室候考。 · 仔细听考试中心的工作人员介绍考前的注意事项。
入场 上午8:00 到 8:30	· 遵照考试中心工作人员的安排在教室外按照考号顺序排队等候。请在排队前先上洗手间。 · 在进入教室前准备好您的身份证和一张护照照片尺寸的彩照待检。彩照必须是6个月内的近照，且背面要写上您的名字和考号。请将您的私人物品存放在指定的区域。 · 根据桌上的标签找到您的位置。 · 请就座。您可以利用这段时间测试一下您的耳机。
准备考试 上午8:30 到 9:00	· 在所有考生就坐后，监考人员会开始宣读考试事项。 · 您的身份证会被暂时集中收起，并在笔试结束前发还给您。 · 监考人员会给您分发听力/阅读答题纸。请根据指示填好答题纸(听力部分和阅读部分的答题区分别在答题纸的正反两面)。 · 根据指示测试您的耳机。 · 监考人员将分发听力试卷并要求您在封面填写姓名和考号。 · 听力考试录音中会提示您何时打开试卷。在此之前，您不可以打开试卷。 · 在考试正式开始以前，监考人员还会要求您再次检查耳机。
考试进行中 上午9:00到12:00	· 考试于早上9:00正式开始。 · 请注意听从监考人员的指示。 · 如果您有疑问，请举手向监考人员示意寻求帮助。 · 如果您认为您得到的试卷有误，或是试卷缺页、模糊，请马上告诉监考人员。 · 在考试进行期间，您不能和其他考生互借文具。 · 当您听到停止作答的指示时，请马上停止答卷，并放下铅笔。否则您将被视为违反考试规则，可能被取消考试成绩。

■ 口试部分

- 请在您预定的口试时间前 30 分钟到达考试中心并签到。未能在考试前 15 分钟到达并签到的考生，将有可能被取消参加口试的资格，并不得转考、退考或退费。
- 请带上您的身份证参加口试。
- 听从工作人员的指挥，在候考室待考。工作人员会带领您到口试考场。请在口试考场外等候考官请您进入。
- 口试考试时间为 11 到 14 分钟。
- 在完成口试后，请立即离开考场。不要与任何人谈及您的考试情况，否则可能会被视做违反考场纪律。

■ 考试建议

- 您可以在考试日前4天从NEEA IELTS 报名网站（http://ielts.etest.net.cn）上查看您的考号和口试时间，并打印准考证。
- 请您在参加考试前仔细阅读《中国地区IELTS考生须知》。
- 请您带上身份证明，一张护照尺寸的6个月内的彩照（照片后面附上您的姓名和考号），以及您的准考证到考场。
- 您在笔试和口试入场前均须出示与报名时一致的有效身份证件，出示与报名信息不符证件的考生将有可能不能参加考试，并不得转考、退考或退费。
- 强烈建议您不要携带手机或其他电子通讯类产品进入考场。所有电子、通讯设备禁止带入考场，即使已呈关闭状态。这一规定同时适用于笔试和口试。任何携带电子、通讯设备进入考场的考生，一律取消考试资格。
- 除了需要检验身份证和照片之外，考生禁止携带任何私人物品进入考场。此规定同时适用于笔试和口试。请不要携带任何贵重物品到考场，考生的个人物品将被存放在考场以外的指定地点。英国文化协会中国办公室（英国驻华使/领馆文化教育处）和考试中心恕不对考生个人物品的损失或遗失负责。

IELTS 测试成绩计算方式

IELTS 测试分为 Listening、Reading、Writing 和 Speaking 四项，此四项皆独立计分，最后再以四个分数合计，除以四而得一平均分数，所以在成绩单上会列出每项的分数和平均分数。IELTS 的满分为 9 分，若成绩达 Band 9，表示该考生能自如地运用英语，具备在英语语言国家学习的能力。反之，若成绩是 Band 1，则表示该考生不具有在英语语言国家学习的英语能力。每所学术机构要求的最低入学成绩不尽相同，一般来说，大部分学校会要求学生至少具备 IELTS 6.0~6.5 或同等程度的入学标准。

■ 计算方式

四大项都有 0.5 分(如 5.5,6.5)。

总分：将四项得分平均后，除 0.5 分外，每 0.25 进一个单位(0.5)

	例一	例二	例三
听力 Listening Band	7.0	6.0	6.0
阅读 Reading Band	6.0	6.0	5.5
写作 Writing Band	6.5	7.0	5.5
口试 Speaking Band	7.5	7.0	5.5
平均	(7.0+6.0+6.5+7.5)/4 =6.75(可进位)	(6.0+6.0+7.0+7.0)/4 =6.5	(6.0+5.5+5.5+5.5)/4 =5.625(不可进位)
总分	7	6.5	5.5

■ 考试成绩与成绩单发放

雅思考试成绩单是考生英语能力的权威证明，显示考生听力、阅读、写作和口语4个分项的成绩以及总成绩。雅思考试成绩自考试之日起2年内有效。

考生须正常完成笔试、口试所有科目并如期参加现场照相方可收到成绩单。考生可以在笔试后第10个工作日登录教育部考试中心雅思报名网站“我的状态”页面查看考试成绩。考生成绩单将同时通过EMS(仅限于中国大陆地区服务)寄往考生报名时提供的成绩单寄送地址，每位考生只能收到1份成绩单原件。

■ 额外成绩单申请与寄送

成绩公布后，考生可以登录雅思官网考后服务平台在线申请寄送额外成绩单并支付相关费用。额外成绩单在线寄送申请一旦提交成功便无法更改或取消。从2012年1月7日起参加考试的考生，雅思成绩2年有效期内申请的前5份额外成绩单寄送将免除人民币60元/份的普通服务手续费用。从第6份额外成绩单起，普通服务手续费为人民币60元/份。

■ 成绩复议

若欲复议成绩，考生需在收到成绩单后，登录“雅思官网考后服务平台”在线申请成绩复议服务，并支付相关费用1000元。同时，还需将成绩单原件寄送到雅思考试全国考后服务热线，收件人是英国大使馆文化教育处考试部。复议服务申请时限为考试日期后6周内。

若复议结果高于原成绩，则复议费用全数退还；若成绩相同或低于原分数，则复议费用不予退还。

IELTS

VOCABULARY FOCUS

常考主题必备词汇

Nature · Environment · Global problems

☑☑☑ 高频单词 Most frequently used vocabulary in the IELTS Test

disastrous
[dɪ'zɑːstrəs]

(a.) 灾害的，灾难性的

The typhoon had a **disastrous** effect on the local economy because it destroyed all the coconut trees.

派 disaster [dɪ'zɑːstər] (n.) 灾难，不幸

catastrophe
[kə'tæstrəfi]

(n.) 大灾难（程度较disaster严重）

Action is urgently required to prevent the disaster from turning into a **catastrophe**.

contaminate
[kən'tæmɪneɪt]

(v.) 污染，弄脏；玷污（亦可指玷污、腐蚀人的思想或品格）

All kitchen staff must wash their hands carefully to remove any germs that may **contaminate** the food.

派 contamination [kənˌtæmɪ(ə)'neɪʃən] (n.) 污染 (= pollution)

chemical
['kemɪkəl]

(a.) 化学的，有化学作用的

Drinking coffee causes us to feel more alert by creating a **chemical** reaction in the brain.

climate
['klaɪmət]

(n.) 气候

The earth's **climate** is getting hotter and drier due to global warming.

dispose
[dɪ'spəʊz]

(v.) 处理掉，销毁

After the project is finished, a crane will be used to **dispose** of all the waste materials.

MP3-003

erosion
[i'rəʊʒən]

(n.) 侵蚀，腐蚀

Due to the threat of **erosion**, it is unsafe to build on the land.

派 erode [ɪ'rəʊd] (v.) 侵蚀

deforestation
[diː,fɒrɪ'steɪʃən]

(n.) 滥伐森林

Deforestation is one of the consequences of our expanding urban areas.

emission
[ɪ'mɪʃən]

(n.) 排放物

The government is considering placing a tax on the carbon **emissions** of each company.

greenhouse
['griːnhaʊs]

(n.) 温室

Tomatoes that are grown in **greenhouses** are able to survive through the winter months.

搭 greenhouse effect 温室效应
greenhouse gas 导致温室效应的气体，如二氧化碳、甲烷等

fossil fuel
['fɒsəl 'fjʊəl]

(n.) 化石燃料（如煤或石油）

Most of the carbon emissions are caused by burning **fossil fuels** such as coal and oil.

blaze
[bleɪz]

(n.) 火灾 (v.) 燃烧

The **blaze** from the bushfire was so hot and intense it burnt everything that stood in its path.

conflagration
[,kɒnflə'greɪʃən]

(n.) 大火灾（正式用语）

The spark from the engine caused a **conflagration** that destroyed almost half of the forest.

consumption
[kən'sʌmpʃən]

(n.) 消耗；消费，用尽

It is imperative that we reduce **consumption** of fossil fuels if we are to halt or reverse global warming.

wildlife
['waɪldlaɪf]

(n.) 野生生物，野生动物

The **wildlife** of Taiwan is rich and diverse.

volcano
[vɒl'keɪnəʊ]

(n.) 火山

It is dangerous to live near an active **volcano** because at any time, without advance notice, it can erupt.

iceberg
['aɪsbɜːg]

(n.) 冰山

It was an **iceberg** which led to the demise of the Titanic.

waterfall
['wɔːtəfɔːl]

(n.) 瀑布

The **waterfall** was very picturesque until the government decided to build a big dam a little way upstream.

equator
[ɪ'kweɪtəʳ]

(n.) 赤道

Typhoons north of the **equator** rotate counterclockwise, while south of the **equator** they are known as cyclones and spin clockwise.

ecosystem
['iːkəʊˌsɪstɪ(ə)m]

(n.) 生态系统

The introduction of civilisation into natural **ecosystems** often has devastating effects.

ecology
[ɪ'kɒlədʒi]

(n.) 生态学

You cannot understand the **ecology** of an area by looking at individual plants and animals.

MP3-004

devastate
[ˈdevəsteɪt]

(v.) 使…毁灭，严重破坏；令人沮丧、震惊

The village **devastated** by floods last year celebrated its recovery with a parade.

devastation
[ˌdevəˈsteɪʃən]

(n.) 毁灭

Bushfires cause mass **devastation** to forests and wildlife every year.

vegetation
[ˌvedʒɪ(ə)ˈteɪʃən]

(n.) [总称] 植物

The **vegetation** in tropical forests is very dense. So much so that in many places you cannot see the sky.

eradication
[ɪˌrædɪ(ə)ˈkeɪʃən]

(n.) 根除，消灭

That humanitarian group's goal is the **eradication** of poverty in all of Africa.

eliminate
[ɪˈlɪmɪ(ə)neɪt]

(v.) 消灭；排除

The effects of pollution are **eliminating** species around the world.

inspection
[ɪnˈspekʃən]

(n.) 调查，检验，视察

The cleanliness of the school cafeteria was so horrible that it didn't pass **inspections**.

bacteria
[bækˈtɪəriə]

(n.) 细菌

Not all **bacteria** is bad for you; in fact, the human body needs **bacteria** for some bodily functions.

rainfall
[ˈreɪnfɔːl]

(n.) 降雨（量）

During the typhoon, the **rainfall** exceeded the amount the city would usually get in one month.

profound
[prə'faʊnd]

(a.) 极深的；涵义深远的

The effects of the earthquake were **profound**. The entire city was damaged in one way or another.

implication
[ˌɪmplɪ(ə)'keɪʃən]

(n.) 牵连；指示，暗示

You need to consider the **implications** of this decision to buy property in the marsh. It is likely that environmental groups will protest against apartments being built on a site they want to become a natural preserve.

派 implicate ['ɪmplɪkeɪt] (v.) 涉及，牵连

terrace
['terɪ(ə)s]

(n.) 台地，梯形丘；阳台

In the mornings I like to eat breakfast on the **terrace** while listening to the birds singing.

surveyor
[sə'veɪə^r]

(n.) 测量员，勘测员

The **surveyor** determined the natural boundaries of the property by using a prism system and GPS.

派 survey ['sɜːveɪ] (n.) [sə'veɪ] (v.) 测量，勘测

channel
['tʃænl]

(n.) 水路；海峡；频道；管道

The **Channel** Tunnel connects England to France.

silicon
['sɪlɪkən]

(n.) 硅

Because **silicon**, as a material, is used a lot in computers, the word '**silicon**' has become another word for the computer industry itself. For example, '**Silicon** Valley' in California is home to a lot of computer-related research and development firms.

MP3-005

exploration
[ˌekspləˈreɪʃən]

(n.) 探测，勘察

A few months ago the legislature signed a law to increase funding for space **exploration**. They hope to send a man to Mars someday!

派 explore [ɪkˈsplɔːʳ] (v.) 探索，考察

astronaut
[ˈæstrənɔːt]

(n.) 航天员

Neil Armstrong was the first **astronaut** to set foot on the moon.

astronomy
[əsˈtrɒnəmi]

(n.) 天文学

She finds **astronomy** very amazing, so one thing her boyfriend did to impress her was to have a star named after her.

invasive
[ɪnˈveɪsɪv]

(a.) 侵略的，入侵的

The **invasive** 'crown of thorns' starfish is seen as a major threat to the Great Barrier Reef.

派 invasion [ɪnˈveɪʒən] (n.) 侵略

preservation
[ˌprezəˈveɪʃən]

(n.) 保存；维护

Historical **preservation** tends to be popular in very rich areas, but I think that there are sites in many poor areas that are also worth preserving.

同 conservation [ˌkɒnsəˈveɪʃən] (n.)（对自然环境的）维护
►conservation area 保护区
maintenance [ˈmeɪntənəns] (n.) 维修，保养
►maintenance staff 维修人员

flooding
[ˈflʌdɪŋ]

(n.) 洪水泛滥，水灾

The river that goes through our town is in danger of **flooding**. If such an event were to happen, it would ruin several shops and houses.

artificial
[ˌɑːtɪ(ə)ˈfɪʃəl]

(a.) 人造的，人工的；虚假的

Artificial reefs are built for the enjoyment of divers and to protect the environment and historically sensitive maritime habitats.

fertility
[fɜːˈtɪlɪ(ə)ti]

(n.) 肥沃；受孕

Global overpopulation may not be an issue if **fertility** rates around the world continue to fall.

fertilise
[ˈfɜːtɪ(ə)laɪz]

(v.) 施肥，使肥沃；使受精

The use of pesticides for **fertilising** crops is quite controversial.

spectacular
[spekˈtækjʊləʳ]

(a.) 壮观的，雄伟的

I heard that the Great Wall of China is a **spectacular** sight to see.

lunar
[ˈluːnəʳ]

(a.) 月亮的；阴历的

Chinese New Year is celebrated at a different time every year depending on the **lunar** calendar.

Celsius
[ˈselsiəs]

(n.)（温度）摄氏

Zero degrees **Celsius** is the temperature that water freezes at.

Fahrenheit
[ˈfærənhaɪt]

(n.)（温度）华氏

Her temperature was 99 degrees **Fahrenheit**, which is above normal but still not considered to be a fever.

horizon
[həˈraɪzən]

(n.) 地平线

Many people at the beach are content to just stare into the **horizon**, where the ocean meets the sky.

MP3-006

landmark
[ˈlændmɑːk]

(n.) 地标
The place where I live actually has many **landmarks**, and one of them is the National Art Palace.

terrestrial
[təˈrestriəl]

(a.) 陆地的；陆栖的；地球的
The **terrestrial** animals can be found in the north, east and central parts of the zoo.

marine
[məˈriːn]

(a.) 海的；海事的；海军的
At the aquarium you can see many different kinds of **marine** life.

shortage
[ˈʃɔːtidʒ]

(n.) 短缺，缺乏；不足（额）
The water **shortage** in our town meant that only once in every three days could a household have access to water.

irrigation
[ˌɪrɪˈgeɪʃən]

(n.) 灌溉
In very dry climates such as that of central Queensland, water **irrigation** is necessary to grow crops.

drought
[draʊt]

(n.) 干旱，久旱不雨
Droughts have a devastating effect on farmers who depend on a regular supply of rain to water their crops.

Antarctica
[ænˈtɑːktɪkə]

(n.) 南极洲
Most species of penguins live in **Antarctica**.

polar
[ˈpəʊləʳ]

(a.) 南北极地的；完全相反的
Because of global warming, the **polar** ice caps are slowly melting.

carbon dioxide
[ˈkɑːbən daɪˈɒksaɪd]

(n.) 二氧化碳

Many scientists agree that **carbon dioxide** is a major cause of global warming.

ultraviolet
[ˌʌltrəˈvaɪəlɪ(ə)t]

(a.) 紫外线的

This lotion is a good product because not only does it make your skin softer, but it also protects your skin from **ultraviolet** rays.

reef
[riːf]

(n.) 沙洲，礁

There are many fascinating sea creatures that can be found in the Great Barrier **Reef** which runs along the eastern coast of Australia.

moisture
[ˈmɔɪstʃər]

(n.) 湿气

The **moisture** in the air is making the car windows foggy.

monsoon
[mɒnˈsuːn]

(n.) 夏季季风期的雨季

During the **monsoon** season, it is best to keep an umbrella with you.

flaw
[flɔː]

(n.) 瑕疵；缺陷

Designer babies have been genetically engineered to make up for nature's **flaws**.

absorb
[əbˈsɔrb]

(v.) 吸收

Cotton is much better at **absorbing** liquids than nylon.

eruption
[ɪˈrʌpʃən]

(n.) 爆发

That volcano has been dormant for over one hundred years, so there is little chance of an **eruption**.

派 erupt [ɪˈrʌpt] (v.) 爆发

MP3-007

organic
[ɔː'gænɪk]

(a.) 生物的；有机的

There is a popular trend towards eating **organic** vegetables rather than chemically produced ones.

rainforest
[reɪn'fɒrɪ(ə)st]

(n.)（热带）雨林

In large parts of Brazil, **rainforests** are slowly being wiped out.

acid rain
['æsɪ(ə)d reɪn]

(n.) 酸雨

Due to the amount of air pollution from the nearby factories, **acid rain** was a common occurrence in the city.

environmentalist
[ɪnˌvaɪərən'mentəlɪ(ə)st]

(n.) 环境保护者

Environmentalists were responsible for the protests against the whaling boats.

hurricane
['hʌrɪ(ə)kən]

(n.) 飓风

The town was completely destroyed after the giant **hurricane** swept through it.

famine
['fæmɪ(ə)n]

(n.) 饥饿；饥荒

Every year, **famine** is the cause of thousands of deaths in African countries.

malnutrition
[ˌmælnjʊ'trɪʃən]

(n.) 营养失调

Due to the drought and food shortages, the villagers soon suffered from **malnutrition**.

slaughter
[ˈslɔːtəʳ]

(v.) (n.) 屠杀

All animals were **slaughtered** in order to provide the village with enough food.

The enemy army were responsible for the mass **slaughter** of all the villagers.

distribution
[ˌdɪstrɪ(ə)ˈbjuːʃən]

(n.) 分布；分支

Due to the continuing drought, the **distribution** of water across the land was limited.

deterioration
[dɪˌtɪəriəˈreɪʃən]

(n.) 退化，衰败；恶化

The development of beachfront property often leads to the **deterioration** of once pristine coastline.

派 deteriorate [dɪˈtɪəriəreɪt] (v.) 恶化

depletion
[dɪˈpliːʃən]

(n.) 消耗，耗尽

The lack of rain for a period of seven months was responsible for the **depletion** of water in the dam.

poisonous
[ˈpɔɪzənəs]

(a.) 有毒的；有害的

Australia is well known for its high population of **poisonous** snakes.

同 toxic [ˈtɒksɪk] (a.) 有毒的，引起中毒的
venomous [ˈvenəməs] (a.)（蛇、蜘蛛等）有毒的；恶毒的，充满仇恨的
noxious [ˈnɒkʃəs] (a.) 有毒的；有害的（正式用语）

industrialise
[ɪnˈdʌstriəlaɪz]

(v.) 使其工业化

It is hoped that the Congo River Dam will help **industrialise** Africa.

派 industry [ˈɪndəstri] (n.) 工业，企业
►sunset industry 夕阳产业
industrialisation [ɪnˌdʌstriəlaɪˈzeɪʃən] (n.) 工业化

MP3-008

agriculture
[ˈæɡrɪˌkʌltʃəʳ]

(n.) 农业

The main industry of developing countries is usually **agriculture**.

☑☑☐ 精选单词 Specialised vocabulary used in the IELTS Test

evolution
[ˌiːvəˈluːʃən]

(n.)（动植物的）演化；进化论

There is no simple explanation for the **evolution** of a species.

/ **human inhabitant**
[ˈhjuːmən ɪnˈhæbɪ(ə)tənt]

(n.) 居民，住民

Places where there are no **human inhabitants** are becoming rarer and rarer throughout the world.

species
[ˈspiːʃiːz]

(n.)（动植物的）物种，种类

The biodiversity of the earth is becoming smaller due to the constant extinction of **species**.

alien species
[ˈeɪliən ˈspiːʃiːz]

(n.) 外来的动植物

The reason that many governments will not allow plants or produce to go through customs is because they do not want an **alien species** to disrupt the natural ecosystem in their country.

creature
[ˈkriːtʃəʳ]

(n.) 生物，动物；创造物

There are many interesting **creatures** in the sea, including dolphins, whales, starfish, seahorses and eels!

/ **radiocarbon**
[ˌreɪdiəʊˈkɑːbən]

(n.) 放射性碳

The age of an artefact as old as this one can only be determined by **radiocarbon** dating.

biodiversity
[ˌbaɪəʊdaɪˈvɜːsɪ(ə)ti]

(n.) 生物多样性

The **biodiversity** of the earth is being threatened by the continued expansion of human settlements and the excessive use of natural resources.

vaporise
[ˈveɪpəraɪz]

(v.) 蒸发

The sun is so hot in the Australian desert that a glass of water **vaporises** in no time.

balmy
[ˈbɑːmi]

(a.) （气候）温暖的

The weather in Southern England is mostly nice and **balmy**. The wind is always a soft breeze and the sun is warm but never too hot.

inadvertently
[ˌɪnədˈvɜːtəntli]

(adv.) 不是有意地；不慎地

The logging of the forest **inadvertently** exposed the remains and artefacts of a once lost culture.

heritage
[ˈherɪ(ə)tɪdʒ]

(n.) 文化传统的继承；遗产

1 out of 48 Australians have German **heritage**.

archaeology
[ˌɑːkiˈɒlədʒi]

(n.) 考古学

The reason he studied **archaeology** in college is because he has dreams of going to faraway countries as an archaeologist to find dinosaur remains.

prehistoric
[ˌpriːhɪˈstɒrɪk]

(a.) 史前时期的

Long before humans evolved, giant, **prehistoric** creatures resembling lizards roamed the world. However, the appetites of these animals—known collectively as dinosaurs—were as large as they themselves were, and this ultimately played a part in their downfall.

MP3-009

artefact
[ˈɑːtɪ(ə)fækt]

(n.) （尤指具有考古价值的）人工制品
The National Palace Museum has many **artefacts** from ancient Chinese dynasties.

pouch
[paʊtʃ]

(n.) 袋，小囊
When a kangaroo's baby is young, the mother kangaroo puts the joey in her **pouch**.

幼兽，指小袋鼠。

galaxy
[ˈɡæləksi]

(n.) 银河系
When you consider how large the Milky Way is, it is simply amazing to consider that there are also countless other **galaxies** in the universe.

torrid
[ˈtɒrɪ(ə)d]

(a.) 酷热的；热情的
In the desert it is important to find ways to escape the **torrid** heat.

estuary
[ˈestʃuəri]

(n.) 河口
Sediment that forms in river **estuaries** is an excellent source of fossils.

lagoon
[ləˈɡuːn]

(n.) 礁湖，海水湖
Because the water in **lagoons** is much calmer, they are a great place to go swimming.

sultry
[ˈsʌltri]

(a.) 极湿热的；撩人的
The weather on the tropical island where we took our vacation was absolutely **sultry**. We hesitated even to leave the hotel room.

nippy
[ˈnɪpi]

(a.) 寒冷的；敏捷的
The air during the winter is a little **nippy**.

topographical
[ˌtɒpəˈgræfɪkəl]

(a.) 地形的；地形学的
I like to visit places that have interesting **topographical** features, like mountains or canyons.

panoramic
[ˌpænəˈrɑːmɪk]

(a.) 全景的，全貌的
In some places in the Rocky Mountain National Park you can see a **panoramic** view of the ranges as they stretch out across the horizon.

peninsula
[pɪ(ə)ˈnɪnsjʊlə]

(n.) 半岛
The **peninsula** juts out into the ocean for 2 miles.

archipelago
[ˌɑːkɪ(ə)ˈpeləgəʊ]

(n.) 群岛
There are many small islands in the **archipelago** north of the main island of Japan.

prairie
[ˈprɛəri]

(n.) 大草原
Most people think that **prairies** are boring because they are so flat, but actually you can find many interesting life forms there.

plain
[pleɪn]

(n.) 平地，平原
After the beautiful drive through the mountains, we were disappointed to come down and see the **plains**.

mountain range
[ˈmaʊntɪ(ə)n reɪndʒ]

(n.) 连接的山丘、山脉
The **mountain range** extending from North-Eastern to South-Eastern Australia is known as 'The Great Dividing Range'.

MP3-010

marsh
[mɑːʃ]

(n.) 沼泽，湿地

Our farm is on the side of a large **marsh**, so our soil is very good for growing crops.

perennial
[pəˈreniəl]

(a.) 多年生的；四季不断的 (n.) 多年生植物

Perennial plants are the easiest to grow because you don't have to replant them every year.

meteorologist
[ˌmiːtiəˈrɒlədʒɪ(ə)st]

(n.) 气象学家

Meteorologists have kept accurate records of weather conditions for over 100 years.

meteorology
[ˌmiːtiəˈrɒlədʒi]

(n.) 气象学

Before **meteorology**, people had very little advance warning of large storms that were on their way over.

methane
[ˈmiːθeɪn]

(n.) 沼气

Methane gas leaks are hard to detect because **methane** is odourless.

amphibian
[æmˈfɪbiən]

(n.) 两栖动物 (a.) 两栖的；水陆两用的

Amphibians such as frogs are fast on both land and water.

chronological
[ˌkrɒnəˈlɒdʒɪkəl]

(a.) 依年代先后顺序排列的

The major natural disasters across history have been recorded in **chronological** order as well as in order of destructive power.

mammal
[ˈmæməl]

(n.) 哺乳动物

Despite the continuing birth of offsprings, the largest sea **mammal** known as the blue whale is under threat of extinction.

☑☐☐ 挑战单词 Sophisticated vocabulary used in the IELTS Test

gulch
[gʌltʃ]

(n.) 两侧高耸且狭窄的峡谷或水道

The **gulch** formed by the Black River has walls so tall that at most times of the day direct sunlight will not get into it.

copse
[kɒps]

(n.) 灌木林，矮树丛

A small **copse** of trees forms a perfect setting for a romantic picnic.

Theme 2

MP3-011

Society

☑☑☑ 高频单词 Most frequently used vocabulary in the IELTS Test

protest
[ˈprəʊtest]
[prəˈtest]

(n.) 反对，抗议 (v.) 反对；声明

The government's new tax policy has unleashed a storm of **protest**.

commute
[kəˈmjuːt]

(n.) (v.) 通勤

Inordinately long **commute** times have become a serious issue in many countries.

corruption
[kəˈrʌpʃən]

(n.) 贪污，贿赂；腐败

Corruption is a primary source of waste, inefficiency and injustice.

welfare
[ˈwelfeəʳ]

(n.) 福利；社会救济 (a.) 福利的

To be a good citizen, one must take an interest in public **welfare**.

reliability
[rɪˌlaɪəˈbɪlɪ(ə)ti]

(n.) 可靠，可信赖

As the job involved meeting many deadlines, **reliability** of employees was a priority.

pursuit
[pəˈsjuːt]

(n.) 追赶；追求

In modern society the **pursuit** of money is increasingly important in order to sustain a comfortable lifestyle.

setback
[ˈsetbæk]

(n.) 挫折；逆境

Failing the university entrance exam was a **setback** to furthering his career.

同 frustration [frʌsˈtreɪʃən] (n.) 沮丧，挫败

antisocial
[ˌæntɪˈsəʊʃəl]

(a.) 不善于社交的；**反社会的**

Technology has been blamed for increasing **antisocial** behaviour.

isolation
[ˌaɪsəˈleɪʃən]

(n.) **隔离，孤立**

Spending too much time on the Internet rather than with real people tends to lead to the problem of social **isolation**.

搭 isolation period（传染病人的）隔离期

派 isolated [ˈaɪsəleɪtɪd] (a.) 孤独的，孤立的 (= lonesome = lonely)

satisfactory
[ˌsætɪ(ə)sˈfæktəri]

(a.) **令人满意的；不错的**

Facilities that cater for the disabled are still not of a **satisfactory** standard.

coordinate
[kəʊˈɔːdɪ(ə)neɪt]

(v.) **协调**

One of the main responsibilities of a tour operator is to **coordinate** travel arrangements between hotels and travel agents.

sophistication
[səˌfɪstɪ(ə)ˈkeɪʃən]

(n.) **世故，老练**

Because of his world travels and important job, John was a man of great intelligence and **sophistication**.

sophisticated
[səˈfɪstɪ(ə)keɪtɪ(ə)d]

(a.) 世故的，老练的；**复杂的**

The techniques that the expert used for solving this economics problem were very **sophisticated** and cannot be understood by a regular person.

/**auspicious**
[ɔːˈspɪʃəs]

(a.) 好兆头的；顺利的；**值得庆贺的**

I would like to thank you all for coming here today to help us celebrate this truly **auspicious** occasion—the launching of the Titanic!

MP3-012

debate
[dɪˈbeɪt]

(n.) 辩论会；争论 (v.) 辩论

Strong **debate** over the construction of the resort was inevitable.

The two political parties **debated** the important issue of healthcare funding into the early hours of the morning.

negotiation
[nɪˌɡəʊʃiˈeɪʃən]

(n.) 协商，谈判

When two people disagree or have different goals, **negotiation** is often required in order to reach some form of agreement.

socialisation
[ˌsəʊʃəlaɪˈzeɪʃən]

(n.) 社会化

The **socialisation** of children at an early age is vital to their later adjustment to adulthood.

urbanisation
[ˌɜːbənaɪˈzeɪʃən]

(n.) 都市化

Expanding industry, aided by improvements in agriculture, has led to increasing **urbanisation** in most societies.

circumstances
[ˈsɜːkəmstænsɪz]

(n.)（实际发生的）状况；环境

Circumstances sometimes prevent us from doing what we would like to do.

collapse
[kəˈlæps]

(n.) 倒塌；崩溃

The **collapse** of the economy of Thailand produced a domino effect in the region.

hostility
[hɒˈstɪlɪ(ə)ti]

(n.) 敌意，敌对状态

The **hostility** between the two countries is making the citizens of both countries very nervous.

discrimination
[dɪˌskrɪmɪ(ə)ˈneɪʃən]

(n.) 差别待遇；**歧视**；辨别力

Racial **discrimination** in any form is now illegal in Australia.

派 discriminate [dɪˈskrɪmɪ(ə)neɪt] (v.) 区分，辨别；歧视

- ►discriminate A from B (between A and B) = distinguish A from B = differentiate A from B 区别A与B，辨别A与B
- ►discriminate against sb 歧视某人

minority group
[maɪˈnɒrɪ(ə)ti gruːp]

(n.) 少数族群

Sydney has many different **minority groups**, including El Salvadorians, Indians, Iranians and Vietnamese.

/**condemn**
[kənˈdem]

(v.) **谴责**；判刑

I don't **condemn** this kind of behaviour. I just feel that it should not be allowed in the workplace.

/**prejudice**
[ˈpredʒədɪ(ə)s]

(n.) **成见，偏见**；歧视

George says that he doesn't have any **prejudice** towards other races, but every time he has a problem, he tends to blame it on people who are not white.

civil rights
[ˈsɪvəl raɪts]

(n.) 公民应有的权利

African-Americans gained many **civil rights** during the 1960's and 1970's, but that doesn't mean that everything is totally fair right now.

harassment
[ˈhærəsmənt]

(n.) 骚扰

Harriet sued her boss for sexual **harassment** after he made several disparaging remarks about her figure.

refugee
[ˌrɛfjʊˈdʒiː]

(n.) 难民

Many **refugees** from the ethnic war in Sudan are seeking refuge in the European Union.

派 refuge [ˈrefjuːdʒ] (n.) 避难所，收容所

MP3-013

outcast
[ˈaʊtkɑːst]

(n.) 被遗弃的人；不被特定团体接纳者

Although Leon was a social **outcast** in high school, he later enjoyed great popularity when he founded a computer software company and became a millionaire.

intimidation
[ɪnˌtɪmɪ(ə)ˈdeɪʃən]

(n.) 威胁，胁迫

Every day the secretary feels like she faces **intimidation**, not only from her boss but also from other secretaries.

spokesman
[ˈspəʊksmən]

(n.) 发言人

The **spokesman** of the charity announced how aid will be distributed to those who have been affected by the recent floods.

petition
[pɪ(ə)ˈtɪʃən]

(n.) 请愿书

More than 1,000 people signed a **petition** to prevent the government from building a new airport in the city's east.

deportee
[ˌdiːpɔːˈtiː]

(n.) 被驱逐出境者

The **deportees** had faced hours of interrogation before being forced to leave the country.

penalty
[ˈpenəlti]

(n.) 惩处；罚款

The **penalty** for smoking on school grounds is two days' suspension.

materialise
[məˈtɪəriəlaɪz]

(v.) (使)具体化；突然出现；实现

He promised that he would send the document by Monday, but it is Friday and it has still not **materialised**.

pension
[ˈpenʃən]

(n.) 退休金，年俸；抚恤金

The only reason that he is still in the army is that in a few years he will be able to retire on a **pension**.

personnel
[ˌpɜːsəˈnel]

(n.) 全体职员；人事部门

Maggie is responsible for ensuring that all hospital **personnel** have been vaccinated.

workforce
[ˈwɜːkfɔːs]

(n.) （一群或全体）劳动者

The **workforce** at our New Zealand plant is very young and mostly female.

proportion
[prəˈpɔːʃən]

(n.) 比例；容积；相称

The **proportion** of males in nursing careers is much lower than that of females.

statistically
[stəˈtɪstɪklɪ]

(adv.) 统计上地；根据过去经验地

Statistically the home team is less likely to win.

self-contained
[self kənˈteɪnd]

(a.) 本身即具有设备或功能的，自给自足的

Some traditional communities try to remain **self-contained** but due to the pressures of modernisation most often fail in this respect.

autonomous
[ɔːˈtɒnəməs]

(a.) 自治的；自发的

The **autonomous** organisation for the homeless operated quite effectively despite being understaffed and underfinanced.

sociable
[ˈsəʊʃəbəl]

(a.) 随和的；好交际的

He is a very **sociable** person and so never turns down an opportunity to meet new people.

MP3-014

racism
[ˈreɪsɪzəm]

(n.) 种族主义

It is getting harder and harder to define **racism** in Australia because even though minorities enjoy full civil rights, they may sometimes lose opportunities based on their race.

/ **formality**
[fɔːˈmælɪ(ə)ti]

(n.)（拘谨的）礼仪规范或言行

There is a high degree of **formality** in Japanese companies.

/ **affirmative**
[əˈfɜːmətɪv]

(a.) 肯定的，赞成的

Affirmative action or otherwise known as positive discrimination in British English has been encouraged in the workforce for quite some time now, however not without controversy.

/ **accreditation**
[əˌkredɪ(ə)ˈteɪʃən]

(n.) 官方认可，授权

Our medical college is accredited by the Australian Medical Association. There are only ten schools in Australia that have this **accreditation**.

hierarchy
[ˈhaɪrɑːki]

(n.) 阶级制度；统治阶级

As with humans, monkeys also have a clear social **hierarchy**.

social security
[ˈsəʊʃəl sɪˈkjʊərɪ(ə)ti]

(n.) 社会福利；社会保险金

The British are increasingly coming to realise that they cannot rely on **social security** to provide for them when they get old.

☑☑☐ 精选单词 Specialised vocabulary used in the IELTS Test

/ **dysfunctional**
[dɪsˈfʌŋkʃənəl]

(a.) 失调的，不正常的

Misbehaving children are often the product of a **dysfunctional** family. malfunction

deprivation
[ˌdeprɪ(ə)ˈveɪʃən]

(n.) 失去，剥夺

In today's fast-moving society, sleep **deprivation** is a common problem for many workers.

/ **apathy**
[ˈæpəθi]

(n.) 冷淡；不感兴趣；对重要之事不作回应

There was widespread **apathy** amongst the students who had failed.

/ **apathetically**
[ˌæpəˈθetɪkli]

(adv.) 不感兴趣地；无动于衷地

When I asked Kelly where she wanted to go for dinner, she shrugged her shoulders **apathetically**.

/ **complacent**
[kəmˈpleɪsənt]

(a.) 自鸣得意的，满足的

Don't become **complacent** about life; you should always strive for more.

observable
[əbˈzɜːvəbəl]

(a.) 看得见的；显著的

There were **observable** changes in his behaviour after his brain surgery.

同 noticeable [ˈnəʊtɪ(ə)səbəl] (a.) 显著的，显而易见的
obvious [ˈɒbviəs] (a.) 明显的，易理解的

/ **ambience**
[ˈæmbiəns]

(n.) 气氛，情调；环境

The **ambience** of the restaurant was perfect for a romantic date. autumosphere.

MP3-015

conformist
[kən'fɔːmɪ(ə)st]

(n.) 顺从者（指遵从特定团体或社会的教义与规范）；因循守旧者

Although you may need to break your comfort zone, being a non-**conformist** in the business world can be quite rewarding and challenging.

constituent
[kən'stɪtʃʊənt]

(n.) 选区的选民；成分

Every month the senator sends a newsletter to his **constituents** informing them of what he is doing for them.

driving force
['draɪvɪŋ fɔːs]

(n.) 驱策力

My love for Thai food was the **driving force** behind my decision to go there on vacation.

sanitary
['sænɪ(ə)təri]

(a.) 合乎卫生与健康的

The cafeteria must meet **sanitary** regulations in order to remain open.

white supremacy
[waɪt sʊ'preməsi]

(n.) 白人优越

In some places in Germany, you can still find people who believe strongly in **white supremacy**, but such an attitude is becoming increasingly rare.

colony
['kɒləni]

(n.) 殖民地

Australia, a former British **colony**, was first used as a place to confine criminals of the lowest order of English society.

派 colonise ['kɒləˌnaɪz] (v.) 开拓殖民地

reclusive
[rɪ'kluːsɪv]

(a.) 独居并与外界隔绝的

The **reclusive** man had lived in the forest by himself for ten years before returning to civilisation.

tenet
[ˈtenɪ(ə)t]

(n.) 信念，教义

One of the principal **tenets** of the Christian faith is to 'love your neighbour as yourself'.

orthodox
[ˈɔːθədɒks]

(a.)（在言行、思想上）被认可的；传统的

Her **orthodox** views on politics were challenged by her classmates.

同 traditional [trəˈdɪʃənəl] (a.) 传统的，习俗的，惯例的
conventional [kənˈvenʃənəl] (a.) 依照惯例的，遵循习俗的

aristocratic
[ˌærɪ(ə)stəˈkrætɪk]

(a.) 贵族的

Mr Dearborn comes from an **aristocratic** family in England, which is why his manners are so refined.

urbane
[ɜːˈbeɪn]

(a.)（尤指男人）行为得体的，温文儒雅的

Sammy was his usual **urbane** and charming self at the cocktail party last Friday night.

□□□ 挑战单词 Sophisticated vocabulary used in the IELTS Test

anomie
[əˈnɒmɪ]

(n.) 因道德沦丧所造成的社会混乱；（个人）因没有目标或理想而引起的失落感、疏离感

The social **anomie** in San Fernando is because of the strength of the pornography industry there.

anomaly
[əˈnɒməli]

(n.) 反常的事物或表现；异常现象，异数

There was an **anomaly** in the professor's data, making his theory dubious.

semblance
[ˈsembləns]

(n.) 外观；相似

Any **semblance** of politeness between the two rivals disappeared when they entered the boxing ring.

MP3-016

Science · Technology

☑☑☑ 高频单词 Most frequently used vocabulary in the IELTS Test

derailment
[ˌdiːˈreɪlmənt]

(n.) 出轨

The **derailment** of the busy rush hour train caused many deaths.

tram
[træm]

(n.) 煤矿车；有轨电车

Although **trams** were a popular form of public transport in the cities of the past, they soon became obsolete.

microchip
[ˈmaɪkrəʊˌtʃɪp]

(n.) 微芯片

Advances in the development of computing technology led to the creation of the **microchip**.

microelectronics
[ˌmaɪkrəʊɪlekˈtrɒnɪks]

(n.) 微电子学

The study of **microelectronics** led him to have a successful career in technical design.

magnet
[ˈmægnɪ(ə)t]

(n.) 磁铁

A large **magnet** was used to load and unload the steel building rods onto the truck.

experimental stage
[ɪkˌsperɪ(ə)ˈmentl steɪdʒ]

(n.) 实验阶段

Research into finding a cure for the disease is only at an **experimental stage**.

malfunction
[mælˈfʌŋkʃən]

(n.) 故障

The **malfunction** of the generator was responsible for the warehouse fire.

precaution
[prɪ'kɔːʃən]

(n.) 预防措施

Necessary **precautions** have been taken in order to prevent another accident.

atomic
[ə'tɒmɪk]

(a.) 原子的

When an atom is divided, it creates **atomic** energy.

emission
[ɪ'mɪʃən]

(n.) 放射（物）

Research into controlling the **emission** of harmful gases into the environment is continuing.

radiation
[ˌreɪdi'eɪʃən]

(n.)（热、光的）放射，辐射（线）

High levels of dangerous **radiation** were expelled after the accident at the nuclear power plant.

genetic
[dʒɪ(ə)'netɪk]

(a.) 遗传（性）的

Because I have a **genetic** predisposition for diabetes, I need to be even more careful of what I eat.

Many diseases are not communicable but rather caused by **genetic** factors.

automation
[ˌɔːtə'meɪʃən]

(n.) 自动化（技术）

If we could replace human workers with **automation**, a lot of labour costs will be saved.

The advent of **automation** in society has allowed humans to enjoy more convenience and leisure time.

mechanic
[mɪ'kænɪk]

(n.) 机械工

The **mechanic**, who fixed my car, has been one for 15 years.

MP3-017

technician
[tek'nɪʃən]

(n.) 技术人员

The laboratory **technicians** are responsible for running the blood tests.

Many nations put great effort into training **technicians** in order to advance their societies.

ecology
[ɪ'kɒlədʒi]

(n.) 生态学

Due to a greater awareness of environmental problems in society, more and more young people are studying **ecology**.

artificial intelligence
[ˌɑːtɪ(ə)'fɪʃəl ɪn'telɪ(ə)dʒəns]

(n.) 人工智能

Many people are afraid that current research into **artificial intelligence** will produce robots that will be smarter than humans.

Many hi-tech companies are presently conducting research on **artificial intelligence** in hopes of creating a computer with the capacity to think like the human brain.

/**ozone layer**
['əʊzəʊn 'leɪə^{r}]

(n.) 臭氧层

The **ozone layer** protects the earth from the sun's harmful rays.

In the past few decades many products containing fluorocarbons have caused damage to the ozone layer which protects us from harmful ultraviolet rays.

vaccine
[ˈvæksiːn]

(n.) 疫苗

This tetanus **vaccine** will prevent you from getting rabies if you happen to be bitten by a dog or any other animal with rabies.

The **vaccine** for smallpox was one of the greatest discoveries of the human race.

interconnect
[ˌɪntəkəˈnekt]

(v.) 使互相联系，使有关联或结合

The Internet makes it possible for people in separate parts of the world to be **interconnected**.

The computer and security system are **interconnected** for greater efficiency.

database
[ˈdeɪtəˌbeɪs]

(n.) 数据库

This **database** contains information about the blood type of those who have donated blood to the Red Cross.

The information of all the company's personnel is contained in the computer system's **database**.

/ **exemplify**
[ɪgˈzemplɪ(ə)faɪ]

(v.) 作为…的范例，（举例）证明

What you just said **exemplifies** exactly why we should not put more money into the space programme.

/ **radioactive**
[ˌreɪdiəʊˈæktɪv]

(a.) 放射性的，辐射的

The waste that comes from nuclear fission processes is dangerous because it is **radioactive**.

The area around the Chernobyl nuclear power plant is still somewhat **radioactive** many years after the accident.

MP3-018

impact
[ˈɪmpækt]

(n.) 打击；冲击；影响

The **impacts** of the events of 9/11 will be felt for many years.

Recent technology has had a big **impact** on all societies around the globe.

virtual reality
[ˈvɜːtʃuəl riˈælɪ(ə)ti]

(n.) 虚拟现实 VR

In the future, **virtual reality** will allow us to experience many things such as rock-climbing without the danger of actually doing it.

indispensable
[ˌɪndɪˈspensəbəl]

(a.) 不可缺少的

The Internet has now become an **indispensable** part of modern life.

tele-conferencing
[ˈteliˌkɒnfərənsɪŋ]

(n.) 视讯会议

Instead of wasting time flying here and there for meetings, our company set up a **tele-conferencing** system to save us time and trouble travelling.

destruction
[dɪˈstrʌkʃən]

(n.) 破坏，毁灭

The **destruction** of the environment seems to be less important than economic security to many nations.

clone
[kləʊn]

(v.)（动植物的）基因复制 (n.)（动植物的）无性繁殖

In Britain a sheep was **cloned** a few years ago, so I imagine they will be able to **clone** a human in just a few more years.

biotechnology
[ˌbaɪəʊtekˈnɒlədʒi]

(n.) 生物科技

Biotechnology has allowed farmers to produce greater yields of crops, thanks to many recent breakthroughs in the field.

component
[kəmˈpəʊnənt]

(n.) 成分；零件

The car is of high quality because every small **component** is carefully crafted.

These companies produce most of the computer **components** for overseas technology companies.

transmission
[trænzˈmɪʃən]

(n.) 传动系统；传达

My car's **transmission** broke down today, so I had to get it towed to the repair shop.

magnetic
[mægˈnetɪk]

(a.) 有磁性的，磁铁的

The new train, which will connect Shanghai to its airport, will use **magnetic** levitation to allow it to run quickly and smoothly on its tracks.

animation
[ˌænɪ(ə)ˈmeɪʃən]

(n.) 动画；热情活泼

Japanese **animation** has not only inspired the **animation** market in other Asian countries, but has also become popular in the United States and elsewhere.

gigabyte
[ˈgɪgəbaɪt]

(n.)（计算机的）千兆字节

The company produced a computer with so many **gigabytes** that it rendered the models of other companies obsolete.

MP3-019

installation
[ˌɪnstəˈleɪʃən]

(n.) 安装，装置；就职

When the **installation** process of this software programme is complete, you can begin downloading music from the Internet.

When you sign up for satellite TV, the **installation** is usually free.

evolve
[iˈvɒlv]

(v.) 演化；逐步形成

I have a hard time believing that human beings **evolved** from apes.

There are still some people who refuse to believe that both humans and monkeys **evolved** from the same ancestors.

hypothesis
[haɪˈpɒθɪ(ə)sɪ(ə)s]

(n.) 假设，臆测

If you are able to prove that your **hypothesis** is correct, you may just have made an important discovery in the field of biochemistry.

同 assumption [əˋsʌmpʃən] (n.) 假定，假设

ideology
[ˌaɪdiˈɒlədʒi]

(n.) 意识形态

The IT company's strong adherence to its **ideology** of success in innovation ensured it was always at the cutting edge of the industry.

net pornography
[net pɔːˈnɒgrəfi]

(n.) 网络色情

The pornography industry was one of the first to take advantage of the conveniences of the Internet. Therefore, **net pornography** has become a serious problem.

Net pornography has become so common that it has become a major social problem in hi-tech societies.

☑☑☐ 高频单词 Specialised vocabulary used in the IELTS Test

amplification
[ˌæmplɪ(ə)fɪ(ə)ˈkeɪʃən]

(n.) 放大；扩大

The **amplification** of sound is necessary at large outdoor musical concerts.

/ **molecule**
[ˈmɒlɪkjuːl]

(n.) 分子；微分子

Hydrogen and oxygen are the two atoms that make up a **molecule** of water.

/ **photosynthesis**
[ˌfəʊtəʊˈsɪnθɪ(ə)sɪ(ə)s]

(n.) 光合作用

In order for green plants to live, the process of **photosynthesis** must take place.

gravity
[ˈgrævɪ(ə)ti]

(n.) 地心引力，重力

Without the natural force of **gravity**, the world would be uninhabitable.

gravitational force
[ˌgrævɪ(ə)ˈteɪʃənəl fɔːs]

(n.) 引力作用

The **gravitational force** of the planets orbiting around the sun allows the earth to receive its much needed sunlight.

meteorology
[ˌmiti(ə)ˈrɒlədʒi]

(n.) 气象学

The scientific study of **meteorology** helps us predict future weather patterns.

spacecraft
[ˈspeɪskrɑːft]

(n.) 宇宙飞船

Billions of US dollars have been spent on improving technology in building NASA **spacecrafts**.

MP3-020

biochemist
[ˌbaɪəʊˈkemɪ(ə)st]

(n.) 生化学家

Recent research into genetically modified animals is being conducted by **biochemists** around the world.

/ **techno-phobe**
[ˈteknəʊ fəʊb]

(n.) 对科技感到恐惧的人

He's a bit of a **techno-phobe**. He always feels intimidated by computers and other new technologies.

/ **cybernetics**
[ˌsaɪbəˈnetɪks]

(n.) 神经机械学

In the world of **cybernetics**, humans can be broken down into parts like a machine.

pharmacology
[ˌfɑːməˈkɒlədʒi]

(n.) 药理学

My friend was more interested in researching medicine, so she studied **pharmacology** instead of going on to medical school to become a doctor.

/ **artisan**
[ˈɑːtɪ(ə)zæn]

(n.) 手工艺者

My grandfather is a very skilled **artisan**. He can make many things out of wood.

When I was in Bangkok, I had the opportunity to visit a village of **artisans** and watch them creating their artwork and crafts.

/ **botany**
[ˈbɒtəni]

(n.) 植物学

From when she was very young, she has always had an interest in nature, so her parents suggested her to study **botany**.

The Amazon Basin provides a vast treasure house for the study of **botany**.

/ **physiology**
[ˌfɪziˈɒlədʒi]

(n.) 生理学

I have always been interested in how the **physiology** of flowers is different from that of ferns.

/ **chromosome**
[ˈkrəuməsəum]

(n.) 染色体

Down's syndrome can be attributed to a certain defect in a person's **chromosome** composition.

The presence of a Y **chromosome** determines that the gender of a human will be male.

diesel-powered
[ˈdiːzəl ˈpauəd]

(a.) 以柴油为引擎动力的

Diesel-powered vehicles tend to have very dark exhaust.

When I was in Germany, I noticed the locals seem to drive more **diesel-powered** vehicles.

/ **ubiquitous**
[juːˈbɪkwɪ(ə)təs]

(a.) 无所不在的

The Internet is making it possible for information to be **ubiquitous**.

hypertext
[ˈhaɪpəˌtekst]

(n.) 超文本，（计算机网页）以关键词链接其搜寻的相关页面

In Microsoft Office Word, you can include **hypertext** links that will send you to certain internet pages.

petroleum
[pɪ(ə)ˈtrəuliəm]

(n.) 石油

Petroleum resources will not last forever. They will run out eventually.

Some of the **petroleum**-producing nations of OPEC are not located in the Middle East.

MP3-021

combustion
[kəm'bʌstʃən]

(n.) 燃烧；氧化

The oil **combustion** engine that cars use was probably one of the greatest inventions ever invented.

The **combustion** system of a car requires fossil fuels but in the future it may just require water.

☑☐☐ 挑战单词 Sophisticated vocabulary used in the IELTS Test

astronavigation
[ˌæstrəʊˌnævɪ'geɪʃən]

(n.) 太空航行，天文导航

Recent research into **astronavigation** has brought about changes in the way we perceive our universe.

spectrometer
[spek'trɔmitə^r]

(n.) 分光计，光谱仪

Scientists use a **spectrometer** to measure the band of coloured lights in a rainbow.

spectrum
['spektrəm]

(n.) 光谱

The rainbow exhibited a beautiful **spectrum** of bright colours across the sky.

meteoroid
['mitɪərˌɔɪd]

(n.) 流（陨）星体

Luckily the **meteoroid** finally broke into small pieces before it hit the earth.

Travel • Culture • Holidays & Festivals

☑☑☑ 高频单词 Most frequently used vocabulary in the IELTS Test

package tour
[ˈpækɪdʒ tʊəʳ]

(n.) 组合套装旅游行程

Tim didn't want the hassles of planning and organising his trip around Europe, so he decided to join a **package tour**. Little did he know the trouble he was getting himself into.

tour guide
[tʊəʳ gaɪd]

(n.) 导游

Mr and Mrs Lee had a wonderful trip to New Zealand, seeing all kinds of strange and wonderful sights. However, the most memorable part of the trip was the exemplary service they received from their **tour guide**, Sally.

flight
[flaɪt]

(n.) 航班，飞行（旅程）

Flight TA567 to Rome has been temporarily delayed due to unforeseen circumstances. Sorry for any inconvenience.

Jill had a lovely **flight**. The service and food were excellent; there was hardly any turbulence and she got to watch her favourite movie 'Sleepless in Seattle'.

flight attendant
[flaɪt əˈtendənt]

(n.) 空服员

The life of a **flight attendant** is not as glamourous as most people think: long-haul flights, irritating passengers and tight schedules make the work a lot harder than it would first seem.

MP3-023

transfer
[træns'fɜː]

(v.) 转机；转移；调职

Flying from Perth to London, we had to **transfer** four times, which made the flight a lot longer.

accommodation
[əˌkɒmə'deɪʃən]

(n.)（短期的）住处，住所

If you plan to travel in China during a national holiday, it is best to book your **accommodation** as early as possible to save the hassle of arriving in a city and not having anywhere to stay.

reservation
[ˌrezə'veɪʃən]

(n.) 预订

Reservations can be made in advance by contacting the tourism information office.

同 booking ['bʊkɪŋ] (n.) 预订

departure
[dɪ'pɑːtʃə^r]

(n.) 启程，出发

The estimated time of **departure** from London Victoria to Leeds is 15:04.

embark
[ɪm'bɑːk]

(v.) 开始；上船

The Jones **embarked** on their road trip across Britain in high spirits. Little did they know the troubles that lay ahead of them.

excursion
[ɪk'skɜːʃən]

(n.) 短程旅行，远足

Every year Miss Smith takes her students on an **excursion** to the zoo to help them learn about the habitats of native and non-native animals.

voyage
['vɔɪ-ɪdʒ]

(n.) 旅行；航行，航海

The **voyage** to Australia across the Indian Ocean is a treacherous one.

long-haul
[lɒŋ hɔːl]

(a.) 长途的

The risk of **long-haul**, intercontinental flights has become more apparent in recent years due to the increase in the number of Deep Vein Thrombosis (DVT) cases on these flights.

deport
[dɪˈpɔːt]

(v.) 驱逐（出境）

After working illegally in Australia on a tourist visa, Paddy McGuire, when discovered, was **deported** immediately to his own country.

repatriate
[ˌriːˈpætrieɪt]

(v.) 回国；把…遣返回国

All immigrants who have entered France should be **repatriated** since immigration was officially stopped in 1974.

embassy
[ˈembəsi]

(n.) 大使馆

In case of loss of passport or travel documents, foreign citizens should proceed to their **embassy** in order to apply for new documentation.

expatriate
[eksˈpætriət]

(n.) 移居国外的人，侨民

The number of **expatriates** coming to live and work in Taipei is increasing at a phenomenal rate.

emigration
[ˌemɪ(ə)ˈgreɪʃən]

(n.) 移居，移民（移出）

Emigration is becoming a major problem for a lot of under-developed countries because skilled, educated citizens leave the country to find better opportunities in more developed places. This has become known as 'brain drain'.

派 emigrant [ˈemɪgrənt] (n.) 移民者（移出至其他国家）

MP3-024

immigration
[ˌɪmɪ(ə)ˈɡreɪʃən]

(n.) **移居，移民**（移入）

Immigration, both legal and illegal, is a perennial source of debate in most societies.

派 immigrant [ˈɪmɪ(ə)ɡrənt] (n.) 移民者（自其他国家移入）

landscape
[ˈlændskeɪp]

(n.) **景色，风景**（尤指乡村）

When I went to Southern Spain, my jaw dropped. The **landscape** was so gorgeous; I thought I was staring at a painting.

ecotourism
[ˈiːkəʊˌtʊərɪzəm]

(n.) **生态之旅**（尤指前往未开发、保存良好的自然环境旅行）

With the growing awareness of the need to protect the natural environment, **ecotourism** has become more and more popular as a means of viewing pristine areas without spoiling them.

relic
[ˈrelɪk]

(n.) **遗骸，遗迹；**因袭旧传统

Many travellers to Italy enjoy visiting museums and historical sites for the great Roman **relics**.

scenery
[ˈsiːnəri]

(n.) **风景，景色；**舞台布景

The **scenery** was lovely. Green trees, a blue lake and snow-capped mountains loomed in the distance.

sightseeing
[ˈsaɪtˌsiːɪŋ]

(n.) **观光，游览**

There are so many places for a tourist to go **sightseeing** that it's hard to know where to start.

souvenir
[ˌsuːvəˈnɪə^{r}]

(n.) **纪念品**

It is always nice, when travelling, to buy small **souvenirs** from different places. Firstly to use as gifts for friends and secondly as a memento of the trip.

skyscraper
['skaɪˌskreɪpəʳ]

(n.) 摩天大楼

Dubai has the tallest **skyscraper** in the world at the moment.

custom
['kʌstəm]

(n.) 风俗，习惯

Unfortunately, fewer and fewer people understand the **customs** and traditions of even their own country.

customs
['kʌstəmz]

(n.) 海关；关税

Customs officials at London Heathrow recently seized a number of endangered species which a man had attempted to hide in his luggage.

expedition
[ˌekspɪ(ə)'dɪʃən]

(n.) 远征，探险（队）；迅速敏捷

This **expedition** was Jack's fifth attempt to climb Mt Everest. All his previous **expeditions** had failed due to extreme weather conditions.

/ **hitchhike**
['hɪtʃhaɪk]

(v.) 搭便车旅行

Hitchhiking is a great way to explore a new country. All that's needed is a sense of adventure, a thumb and the time and patience to stand on the side of the road to wait for someone to stop and give you a lift.

/ **itinerary**
[aɪ'tɪnərəri]

(n.) 旅行计划，预定行程

When travelling, it is always better to have a flexible **itinerary** to allow for any unexpected changes.

stopover
['stɒpˌəʊvəʳ]

(n.)（旅途中的）中途停留

I've only been to Tokyo once. Unfortunately it was a short **stopover** on my way back to London, so I wasn't able to see much.

MP3-025

claim
[kleɪm]

(n.) (v.) 要求；声明

Patrick's luggage was lost on route from Beijing, so after arriving in Sydney he had to make a lost luggage **claim** at the airport.

jetlag
[ˈdʒetlæg]

(n.) 时差

When travelling on long-distance flights, it is best not to drink coffee and alcohol but to drink a lot of water, thereby keeping the body hydrated and reducing the effects of **jetlag**.

luggage
[ˈlʌgɪdʒ]

(n.) 行李

I always try to travel light and not to take too much **luggage**.

terminal
[ˈtɜːmɪ(ə)nəl]

(n.)（机场、火车站、渡口的）等候室；终点站

Before you can enter the airport **terminal**, you must pass a security checkpoint.

full board
[fʊl bɔːd]

(n.) 全食宿服务（旅馆等供应住宿及三餐）

It's quite common for people on working holiday visas to get a job as an au pair as it not only includes **full board** and keep but the money earned will also cover some of their travelling expenses.

chambermaid
[ˈtʃeɪmbəmeɪd]

(n.) 旅馆、饭店的女清洁员

The **chambermaid** was very busy cleaning rooms because the hotel had been fully booked for the whole summer.

porter
[ˈpɔːtə(r)]

(n.) 帮忙旅客搬运行李的服务人员；〈英〉门房

The **porter** helped Mr Jones carry his luggage from the hotel lobby to his room.

/ **certificate of disembarkation**
[sə'tɪfɪkət əv ˌdɪsembɑːˈkeɪʃən]

(n.) 入境证

To save time and hassles going through customs, it is best to fill in the **certificate of disembarkation** and have your passport and visa ready.

altitude
[ˈæltɪ(ə)tjuːd]

(n.) 高度，海拔高度

Fifteen minutes after take-off, the plane reached its cruising **altitude** and the flight attendants started serving drinks.

/ **carousel**
[ˌkærəˈsel]

(n.) 行李转盘、输送带；旋转木马

While Henry was waiting for his luggage at the **carousel**, he suddenly realised that he had forgotten his briefcase on the aeroplane.

connecting flight
[kəˈnektɪŋ flaɪt]

(n.) 接驳班机

When Phil's flight landed in Bangkok, he had to disembark the plane as fast as possible and run to Gate 5 so he could make his **connecting flight** to Kathmandu.

declare
[dɪˈkleə^{r}]

(v.) 申报；宣布；声称

You have to **declare** any animal or plant products you bring into Australia.

destination
[ˌdestɪ(ə)ˈneɪʃən]

(n.) 目的地；终点

We have a number of **destinations** on our European express tour. The first one is London and the final one is Madrid.

domestic flight
[dəˈmestɪk flaɪt]

(n.) 国内班机

Most people in Perth prefer to take their vacation in Bali because **domestic flights** are so expensive in Australia, and flying to Bali is cheaper.

MP3-026

economy
[ɪˈkɒnəmi]

(n.) 经济情况；节省

Economy class is the cheapest type of ticket. Alternatively, business class and first class are available, but at a substantially higher price.

搭 economy class 经济舱
派 economic [ˌiːkəˈnɒmɪk] (a.) 经济上的，经济学的
economical [ˌiːkəˈnɒmɪkəl] (a.) 节俭的；经济实惠的

estimated time of arrival
[ˈestɪ(ə)meɪtɪd taɪm əv əˈraɪvəl]

(n.) 预计到达时间

The pilot announced that the **estimated time of arrival** would be in another 2 hours.

evacuation
[ɪˌvækjuˈeɪʃən]

(n.) 逃生，疏散；撤离

After the **evacuation** of the archaeological site, it will be open for public inspection with the majority of visitors expected to be foreign tourists.

/ **entree**
[ˈɒntreɪ]

(n.) 〈英〉前菜；〈美〉主菜；入场许可

Travelling first class is great, especially the food, as it's not just a meal but includes **entree** and dessert.

inspector
[ɪnˈspektəʳ]

(n.) 检查员，督察

Flight safety **inspectors** need to be very thorough with their investigations, otherwise it may result in fatalities.

/ **layover**
[ˈleɪəʊvəʳ]

(n.)（旅途中）中途停留 stopover

During my **layover** in Singapore, I chose to take advantage of some of the best shopping malls in the world, right at the Singapore airport.

同 stopover [ˈstɒpˌəʊvəʳ] (n.) 中途停留

/ **cosmopolitan**
[ˌkɒzməˈpɒlɪ(ə)tən]

(a.) 国际性的，具有世界各地生活经验的

Frederic is so **cosmopolitan**. He knows what to wear, eat, say, and has no problems mingling in Paris, London and New York.

mingle: 与…交往，相交往

/ **resort**
[rɪˈzɔːt]

(n.) 度假地

Getting fired was the last straw. Helen was fed up and had had enough. She packed her bags and got on the next flight to a small **resort** on an island in the Caribbean.

countryside
[ˈkʌntrisaɪd]

(n.) 郊外，乡间

What a lovely day! Let's go for a drive in the **countryside** and have a quiet picnic in a field with some cows and geese.

feast
[fiːst]

(n.) 盛宴；大餐

After the Thanksgiving **feast**, all I could do was lie on the couch and take a nap.

/ **ornament**
[ˈɔːnəmənt]

(n.) 装饰品

They like to hang the **ornaments** on the Christmas tree together as a family.

/ **indigenous**
[ɪnˈdɪdʒənəs]

(a.) 本土的

It's very important to educate children on their country's **indigenous** culture.

multinational
[ˌmʌltɪˈnæʃənəl]

(a.) 多国的，跨国企业的

The work culture at that **multinational** company is very serious and professional.

MP3-027

ancestry
[ˈænsestri]

(n.) 家世，血统

His **ancestry** can be traced all the way back to the first Spanish colonialists.

ancestral
[ænˈsestrəl]

(a.) 家族的，祖传的

The last time he went to visit his **ancestral** home was twenty years ago.

spectacular
[spekˈtækjʊləʳ]

(a.) 壮观的，蔚为奇观的

The fireworks show was absolutely **spectacular**.

fantastic
[fænˈtæstɪk]

(a.) 惊人的，了不起的

According to visitors, the services offered by the travel agent were absolutely **fantastic**.

marvellous
[ˈmɑːvələs]

(a.) 不可思议的，极好的

The journey offers a **marvellous** opportunity for tourists to encounter and converse with local inhabitants.

magnificent
[mægˈnɪfɪ(ə)sənt]

(a.) 壮丽的，宏伟的

The surrounding countryside has been described as one of the most **magnificent** areas of natural beauty.

breathtaking
[ˈbreθteɪkɪŋ]

(a.) 令人惊艳的

Watching the sun rays glistening over the swaying ocean's silvery surface was simply **breathtaking**.

exhilarating
[ɪgˈzɪləreɪtɪŋ]

(a.) 令人振奋的，使人高兴的

The white water rafting trip down the river rapids was absolutely **exhilarating**.

派 exhilarate [ɪgˈzɪləreɪt] (v.) 使振奋，使高兴

meander
[mi'ændəʳ]

(v.) **漫步，闲逛** (n.) 河流、道路的蜿蜒曲折；漫步

Couples can spend the afternoon **meandering** around the old streets of the town.

同 stroll [strəʊl] (v.) (n.) 漫步，闲逛
wander ['wɒndəʳ] (v.) (n.) 闲逛，徘徊

monument
['mɒnjʊmənt]

(n.) **纪念碑；**遗址

The Statue of Liberty is one of the most famous and frequently visited modern **monuments** in America.

congestion
[kən'dʒestʃən]

(n.) **拥塞，挤满**

Increasing **congestion** on Britain's main motorways has led to a rise in pollution levels.

派 congested [kən'dʒestɪd] (a.) 挤满的，交通堵塞的

heroic
[hɪ'rəʊɪk]

(a.) 英雄的；**英勇的**

The story of **heroic** Hercules which has been passed down the generations is an important part of Greek and Roman culture and has even been made into a kid's movie by Disney.

misfortune
[mɪs'fɔːtʃən]

(n.) 灾祸；**不幸**

We had the **misfortune** of rain throughout our entire honeymoon on the tropical island of Tahiti.

trolley
['trɒli]

(n.) 手推车；电车；**轨道电车**

If you ever get the chance to ride a **trolley** in San Francisco, you should certainly take it.

kiosk
['kiːɒsk]

(n.) 亭；**书报摊**

The bus schedules can usually be found at the **kiosks**.

MP3-028

boutique
[buː'tiːk]

(n.) 流行精品店

I enjoy going to her **boutique** because she is always busy making the most interesting looking clothes.

arcade
[ɑː'keɪd]

(n.) 拱廊；拱廊式商街

That amusement park not only has roller coasters and a mini-golf course, but also an **arcade**.

auction
['ɔːkʃən]

(v.) (n.) 拍卖

There are many famous paintings being **auctioned** off today at that **auction** house.

bid
[bɪd]

(n.) (v.) 出价，投标

Before you place a **bid** on this painting, you must consider how much you can afford and what your highest ultimate **bid** will be.

venue
['venjuː]

(n.) 集合地点，会场

An outside auditorium would be the most suitable **venue** for this concert.

kayaking
['kaɪækɪŋ]

(n.) 划独木舟、小皮艇

At camp you have many options for getting into the water, including swimming, canoeing and **kayaking**.

launch
[lɔːntʃ]

(v.) 使船下水

Going out on the lake is very popular today. Look at the long line of cars waiting to **launch** their boats!

rucksack
['rʌksæk]

(n.)（常指旅行或登山用的）背包

His **rucksack** is packed with enough food supplies to last a week.

adversity
[əd′vɜːsɪ(ə)ti]

(n.) 困境，逆境

Many cultures celebrate those who overcome **adversity** and go on to be great leaders in their field.

religious ceremony
[rɪ′lɪdʒəs ′serɪ(ə)məni]

(n.) 宗教仪式

I find it very interesting to watch the **religious ceremonies** of other religions.

Taoism
[′taʊɪzəm]

(n.) 道教

Taoism is a Chinese religion which has many different gods.

Islam
[′ɪslɑːm]

(n.) 伊斯兰教

It is unfair to associate **Islam** with terrorist acts performed by Muslims.

aboriginal
[ˌæbə′rɪdʒɪ(ə)nəl]

(n.) 原住民 (a.) 原住民的，原始的

Most **aboriginals** in Taiwan live in the mountainous parts of the island.

bamboo rice
[bæm′buː raɪs]

(n.) 竹筒饭

One of my favourite Chinese foods is **bamboo rice**.

culture shock
[′kʌltʃəʳ ʃɒk]

(n.) 文化冲击

One of the first times I realised I was experiencing **culture shock** in China was when I tried ordering food at a restaurant and ended up with pigs' intestines.

gorgeous
[′gɔːdʒəs]

(a.) 美丽且令人愉快的

The Balinese dancers wore **gorgeous** outfits for their performance.

MP3-029

cathedral
[kə'θiːdrəl]

(n.) 教区总教堂，大教堂

When I go to Europe, I want to visit some of the historical **cathedrals** there.

exquisite
[ɪk'skwɪzɪ(ə)t]

(a.) 精致的，精美的

The ceiling of that temple was made completely by hand with no nails. It is absolutely **exquisite**.

Catholic
['kæθəlɪk]

(a.) 天主教的 (n.) 天主教徒

There is a current controversy in the **Catholic** church regarding the shortage of priests.

Easter
['iːstə^r]

(n.) 复活节

Easter is the holiday when Christians celebrate Jesus Christ's resurrection from the dead.

attraction
[ə'trækʃən]

(n.) 吸引力，魅力；景点

The most popular **attraction** at Disneyland is Splash Mountain.

派 attractive [ə'træktɪv] (a.) 诱人的，有吸引力的
attract [ə'trækt] (v.) 吸引
►be attracted by sb/sth = be captivated by sb/sth 被…吸引、迷住

stadium
['steɪdiəm]

(n.)（设有观众席的）露天运动场

Greece built a number of new **stadiums** for the 2004 Olympics.

carnival
['kɑːnɪ(ə)vəl]

(n.) 嘉年华会

The **carnivals** held across Brazil in February every year are most popular for their dancing, costumes and all-night parties.

heyday
['heɪdeɪ]

(n.) 全盛时期

In their **heyday**, the Beatles would have stadiums packed to capacity with audiences of over 100,000 people.

validity date
[və'lɪdɪ(ə)ti deɪt]

(n.) 有效日期

You should check the **validity date** of your passport to ensure you don't get turned away at the airport.

commemorate
[kə'meməreɪt]

(v.) 庆祝；为…举行纪念活动

Americans **commemorated** the anniversary of September 11th by holding a number of solemn ceremonies in their hometowns.

☑☑☐ 精选单词 Specialised vocabulary used in the IELTS Test

jack-o'-lantern
[ˌdʒæk ə 'læntən]

(n.)（万圣节的）南瓜灯笼

Little John took hours choosing the right pumpkin. This Halloween, he was going to carve the biggest and scariest **jack-o'-lantern** in town.

Ramadan
['ræmədæn]

(n.) 斋月（伊斯兰教历的九月）

During **Ramadan**, it may be hard to find any restaurants open.

Sabbath
['sæbəθ]

(n.) 安息日

How much a Jewish person decides to do on the **Sabbath** is often dependant on how strict his/her beliefs are.

posterity
[pɒ'sterəti]

(n.) 后代；子孙

The great leader had a larger than life statue built of himself for **posterity**.

MP3-030

render
[ˈrendər]

(v.) 导致；给予；翻译

New high-speed railway networks have **rendered** the old traditional lines obsolete.

medieval
[ˌmediˈiːvəl]

(a.) 中世纪的

This museum is having a showing of **medieval** art next month.

bazaar
[bəˈzɑːr]

(n.) 义卖市场；市集

You can find many inexpensive but beautiful things at the **bazaar** in the middle of town.

tawdry
[ˈtɔːdri]

(a.) 俗丽的，廉价的

The **tawdry** bars of the red light district were quite popular with the foreign businessmen.

wayfarer
[ˈweɪˌfeərər]

(n.) 徒步旅行者

The **wayfarer** had come all the way from the other side of the country.

berth
[bɜːθ]

(n.) 火车、船的卧铺；停泊处

The marina has enough **berths** to fit 100 boats.

filial piety
[ˈfɪliəl ˈpaɪəti]

(n.) 孝道

Filial piety is a very important value in Chinese society. Traditionally the next generation would mourn their parents for a number of years after they passed away.

reincarnation
[ˌriːɪnkɑːˈneɪʃən]

(n.) 投胎转世，轮回

The Buddhist belief in **reincarnation** is that who or what you become in your next life is dependant on your actions in this one.

adherent
[əd′hɪərənt]

(n.) 拥护者；追随者

He has long been an **adherent** of airline safety.

amenity
[ə′miːnɪ(ə)ti]

(n.) 娱乐设施

The resort's **amenities** were among the best in the country, including a massive pool, fully-equipped gym and even a nightclub and casino.

parish
[′pærɪʃ]

(n.) 教区

The Catholics in my aunt's **parish** tend to be more open-minded than those where I live.

meditation
[ˌmedɪ(ə)′teɪʃən]

(n.) 沉思，冥想

Meditation is becoming a popular alternative for people stressed out by modern societies' pressures.

enlightenment
[ɪn′laɪtənmənt]

(n.) 启发，开导；启蒙

He meditates day and night in the hope that he will be able to achieve **enlightenment**.

☑☐☐ **挑战单词 Sophisticated vocabulary used in the IELTS Test**

UNHCR
[ˌjuːenˌeɪtʃsiː′ɑːʳ]

(n.) 联合国难民总署

UNHCR is the acronym for the United Nations High Commission for Refugees, a United Nations agency that provides for humanitarian and political refugees around the world.

galley
[′gæli]

(n.)（船上或飞机上的）厨房

The flight attendant asked the passenger to leave the **galley** as they were about to encounter turbulence.

MP3-031

endemic
[en'demɪk]

(a.)（尤指疾病）**地方性的，某地特有的**
The tour guide advised us to stay away from certain areas of the city at night as crime was **endemic** there.

■ 补充单词：重要节日

- Valentine's Day 情人节（2月14日）
- Labour Day 劳动节（5月1日）
- Halloween 万圣节前夕（10月31日）
- Thanksgiving Day 感恩节（11月第4个周四）
- Christmas Day 圣诞节（12月25日）
- Edinburgh Art Festival 爱丁堡艺术节（8月）
- St Patrick's Day 圣帕特里克日〔爱尔兰民族节日〕（3 月17日）
- the Lantern Festival 元宵节（农历 正月15日）
- the Tomb Sweeping Festival 清明节（农历 4 月 5日左右）
- the Dragon Boat Festival 端午节（农历5月5日）
- the Moon Festival 中秋节（农历8月15日）

MP3-032

Health

☑☑☑ 高频单词 Most frequently used vocabulary in the IELTS Test

circulation
[ˌsɜːkjʊˈleɪʃən]

(n.)（气体，液体）环流；（血液）**循环**；（货币）流通，发行量

Her **circulation** is poor; hence she suffers from cold extremities in winter.

arthritis
[ɑːˈθraɪtɪ(ə)s]

(n.) 关节炎

Arthritis is a debilitating condition that is most prevalent in persons over the age of 50.

infection
[ɪnˈfekʃən]

(n.) 传染（病）；**感染**

Chest **infections** are more common in damp cold climates than in dry cold ones.

stiffness
[ˈstɪfnəs]

(n.) 严格；不自然；**僵硬**

Stiffness of the joints is more common in winter than in summer.

cholesterol
[kəˈlestərɒl]

(n.) 胆固醇

Many people these days are worried about their **cholesterol** levels.

inflammation
[ˌɪnfləˈmeɪʃən]

(n.) 发炎

The **inflammation** of my gums is unbearable.

stressful
[ˈstresfəl]

(a.) 充满压力的

At the top of the list of **stressful** occupations is that of air traffic controllers.

MP3-033

incurable
[ɪn'kjʊərəbəl]

(a.) 无法治愈的，无药可救的

Despite modern medical advances, a number of diseases remain **incurable**.

protein
['prəʊtiːn]

(n.) 蛋白质

Meat is one of the best sources of **protein** available.

tablet
['tæblɪ(ə)t]

(n.) 药片；一小块木头或坚硬物质；片

The **tablets** should be taken as directed by your physician.

symptom
['sɪmptəm]

(n.) 症状；征兆

If the **symptoms** persist, please consult your medical practitioner.

substance
['sʌbstəns]

(n.) 物质；主旨

The essential **substances** in a proper diet are lots of fruits and vegetables.

treatment
['triːtmənt]

(n.) 处理（方式）；治疗（法）

Psychiatry deals with mental illnesses and their **treatment**.

disorder
[dɪs'ɔːdəʳ]

(n.) 混乱，失序；（身体，精神）不适

Eczema is a **disorder** of the skin.

prevent
[prɪ'vent]

(v.) 预防；阻止

Regular exercise and a healthy diet are the best way to **prevent** disease and maintain a high level of fitness.

high-risk
[haɪ rɪsk]

(a.) 高危险（群）的

Due to chain smoking and excessive drinking, John was a **high-risk** candidate for developing cardiovascular and respiratory problems.

prescription
[prɪˈskrɪpʃən]

(n.)（医生开的）处方；疗法

Having finished her last dose of medication early one Sunday morning, Dora had an anxious 24-hour wait before she could get a new **prescription** from her doctor.

派 prescribe [prɪˈskraɪb] (v.) 开处方

diabetes
[ˌdaɪəˈbiːtiːz]

(n.) 糖尿病

Barry's mother was always very careful not to let him eat too many sweets as a child to prevent him from developing **diabetes** in his old age.

physician
[fɪ(ə)ˈzɪʃən]

(n.)（内科）医生

Fewer and fewer people are willing to become medical **physicians** due to the high rate of litigation in the medical industry.

aspirin
[ˈæsprɪ(ə)n]

(n.) 阿司匹林

It has been discovered that **aspirin** is not only effective for curing headaches but also thins the blood, which is useful for reducing the chance of heart attacks and strokes.

dietician
[ˌdaɪəˈtɪʃən]

(n.) 饮食学家，营养学家

Before starting a diet to lose weight, it is always best to consult a **dietician** to ensure the new diet will have no harmful effects on your health.

MP3-034

pharmacy
[ˈfɑːməsi]

(n.) 药房；配药处；药学

After getting a new prescription from her doctor, Dora went straight to the **pharmacy** to get her new medication.

ward
[wɔːd]

(n.) 病房；牢房；行政区，选区；被监护人（尤指小孩）

When Barry started to threaten other patients and staff in the psychiatric **ward** with erratic, aggressive behaviour, his doctor was forced to relocate him to the isolation **ward** until his condition improved. warden. 监狱长

health insurance
[helθ ɪnˈʃʊərəns]

(n.) 健康保险

The necessity of **health insurance** can only be truly appreciated once a person has had a major health problem and is faced with huge medical expenses.

compulsory insurance
[kəmˈpʌlsəri ɪnˈʃʊərəns]

(n.) 强制险

The move by the government to introduce **compulsory** health **insurance** has angered human rights activists who believe that such a move will disadvantage low-income earners and reduce the standards of the current healthcare system.

hypnosis
[hɪpˈnəʊsɪ(ə)s]

(n.) 催眠术；催眠状态

John decided to try **hypnosis** as a cure for his insomnia only after all the other treatments were found to be either ineffective or unsatisfactory.

subconscious
[sʌbˈkɒnʃəs]

(a.) 潜意识的 (n.) 潜意识

Some people believe that dreams are a manifestation of the **subconscious** mind trying to express itself in a person's conscious life.

theoretical
[θɪəˈretɪkl]

(a.) 理论上的，推论的

From a **theoretical** perspective, this problem would seem easily solved, but practical limitations of the theory make the solution a lot more difficult.

experimental
[ɪkˌsperɪ(ə)ˈmentl]

(a.) 实验的；试验性的

The drug is still at an **experimental** stage so it will not receive government approval until further experiments have been completed.

stimulation
[ˌstɪmjʊˈleɪʃən]

(n.) 刺激，兴奋

The **stimulation** Jack got from drinking three cups of coffee caused him to stay up all night.

派 stimulus [ˈstɪmjʊləs] (n.) 刺激物，激励因素
stimulate [ˈstɪmjʊleɪt] (v.) 激发，促进
►stimulate sb to do sth 激励某人做某事
stimulating [ˈstɪmjʊleɪtɪŋ] (a.) 振奋人心的，令人兴奋的

sensation
[senˈseɪʃən]

(n.) 感觉，知觉；兴奋

After falling from a horse and severing his spinal cord, Barry lost all the **sensation** in his body from his waist down.

anxiety disorder
[æŋˈzaɪəti dɪsˈɔːdər]

(n.) 焦虑症

A number of leading psychologists believe there has been an increase in the number of people diagnosed with **anxiety disorders**.

MP3-035

addiction
[əˈdɪkʃən]

(n.)（吸毒或喝酒）成瘾；**（对某事）上瘾；**沉溺

John had developed a debilitating **addiction** to coffee, resulting in severe anxiety attacks when he didn't have a cup of coffee in his hand.

派 addict [ˈædɪkt] (n.) 成瘾者（尤指吸毒）
►a drug addict 吸毒成瘾者
addicted [əˈdɪktɪd] (a.) 着迷的，上瘾的
►be addicted to sth 对…着迷

obsess
[əbˈses]

(v.) 着迷，缠扰；使身心困扰；**挂念**

It is difficult to focus on daily activities when you start to **obsess** about one problem in your life.

outgrow
[aʊtˈgrəʊ]

(v.) 快速成长；**因长大、变大而不再适用**

As the baby was feeding and sleeping well, it soon **outgrew** all the 0 sized clothes that were given to her at birth.

urge
[ɜːdʒ]

(n.) **强烈欲望，需求，冲动** (v.) 催促，驱策

After being on a diet for only three days, Betty started to have all sorts of **urges**, which she could not control. In the end she had to give in and eat all the chocolate she had stashed under her bed.

dietary
[ˈdaɪətəri]

(a.)（有关）**饮食的**

After he was diagnosed with diabetes, the doctor recommended a number of **dietary** restrictions.

breakdown
[ˈbreɪkdaʊn]

(n.)（身心）**崩溃**；中断（break down 指机器故障或汽车抛锚）

The stress caused by her parents' divorce and not being accepted into her top-choice college caused her to have a psychological **breakdown**.

inherit
[ɪn'herɪ(ə)t]

(v.) 继承（传统，财产）；**遗传**（性格或身体方面的特质）

It's just as likely for children to **inherit** eczema from their father as it is from their mother according to the latest research.

eczema: 湿疹

派 inheritance [ɪn'herɪ(ə)təns] (n.) 遗产（尤指个人财产）
►inheritance tax 遗产税

参 bequest [bɪ'kwest] (n.) 遗产（尤指个人财产）
heritage ['herɪtɪdʒ] (n.) 遗产（尤指社会国家的历史文化传统）

insomnia
[ɪn'sɒmniə]

(n.) 失眠

My work is so stressful that it's causing me to lose sleep. If this **insomnia** continues, I will have to see a doctor.

hormone
['hɔːməʊn]

(n.) 荷尔蒙

Hormone replacement therapy has been used for relief of menopausal symptoms.

hypertension
[ˌhaɪpə'tenʃən]

(n.) 高血压

Regular exercise and a healthy diet is the best cure for **hypertension**.

obesity
[əʊ'biːsɪ(ə)ti]

(n.) 肥胖，肥大

Obesity is becoming more and more of a problem in developed countries.

wakefully
['weɪkfəlɪ]

(adv.) 清醒地；警觉地

The patient found it hard to **wakefully** watch TV while confined to his hospital bed as he had taken so many prescription drugs.

MP3-036

insulin
[ˈɪnsjʊlɪ(ə)n]

(n.) 胰岛素

If your pancreas doesn't secrete a sufficient amount of **insulin**, you need to supplement it with **insulin** shots.

☑☑☐ 精选单词 Specialised vocabulary used in the IELTS Test

cardiovascular
[ˌkɑːdiəʊˈvæskjʊləʳ]

(a.) 心血管的

Cardiovascular disease is becoming common in metropolitan cities.

strain
[streɪn]

(n.) 压力，紧张 (v.) 加重；扭伤；使（液体与固体）分离

He has been under a lot of nervous **strain** since the breakup of his marriage.

holistic
[həʊˈlɪstɪk]

(a.) 整体的，全面的

Holistic approaches to medicine can complement conventional approaches.

compound
[ˈkɒmpaʊnd]

(n.) 化合物 (a.) 复合的，合成的，化合的

Compounds are isolated from plants to produce pharmaceuticals.

paradoxical
[ˌpærəˈdɒksɪkəl]

(a.) 似是而非的，自相矛盾的

There's something **paradoxical** about fast food companies promoting a healthy diet and lifestyle.

同 contradictory [ˌkɒntrəˈdɪktəri] (a.) 相互矛盾的，对立的
ambivalent [æmˈbɪvələnt] (a.)（对某人或某事物）有好坏参半的矛盾看法的

paediatrician
[ˌpiːdiəˈtrɪʃən]

(n.) 小儿科医生

Craig loved children, so after finishing his medical degree he decided to specialise in paediatrics and become a **paediatrician**.

psychotherapy
[ˌsaɪkəʊˈθerəpi]

(n.) 心理疗法，精神疗法

After years of **psychotherapy** which involved exploring Jack's deepest unconscious urges and desires, he was finally proclaimed mentally fit and allowed to be released from solitary confinement to live a normal life with the rest of his fellow inmates.

pacifying
[ˈpæsɪ(ə)faɪɪŋ]

(a.) 使感到平静的，抚慰的

Peter's peaceful approach to the situation had a **pacifying** effect on everyone involved and helped avoid any further violence.

派 pacify [ˈpæsɪfaɪ] (v.) 使平静，抚慰

induce
[ɪnˈdjuːs]

(v.) 劝诱；引导

Once in a while it may be OK to take pills to **induce** sleep, but you have to be careful not to become addicted to them.

gene abnormalities
[dʒiːn ˌæbnɔːˈmælɪ(ə)tɪs]

(n.) 基因突变

Gene abnormalities can cause genetic illnesses such as Down's syndrome.

☑☐☐ 挑战单词 Sophisticated vocabulary used in the IELTS Test

vaccination
[ˌvæksɪ(ə)ˈneɪʃən]

(n.) 接种

If you are travelling to certain parts of Africa or South-East Asia, you will require a **vaccination** against certain diseases.

派 vaccinate [ˈvæksɪ(ə)neɪt] (v.) 给…接种疫苗
（通常使用被动语态 be vaccinated）

MP3-037

sanatorium
[ˌsænəˈtɔːriəm]

(n.) 疗养院

Richard's doctor advised him to check into the local **sanatorium** to facilitate a faster recovery from his latest bout of dysentery.

polyclinic
[ˌpɒliˈklɪnɪk]

(n.) 综合医院，联合诊所

Brendan enjoyed his weekly visit to the local **polyclinic**. Not only did he learn a lot of interesting information about how to control his disease, he had also made a lot of new friends who had a multitude of rare and interesting diseases.

tomography
[təʊˈmɒgrəfi]

(n.)【医】断层扫描

X-ray, ultrasound, PET and MRI are all forms of **tomography** because they are all used to take pictures of the interior of the body.

endocrine
[ˈendəʊkrɪn]

(n.) 内分泌；激素

The **endocrine** system is responsible for gland secretions.

■ 补充单词：常见疾病

- chronic disease [ˈkrɒnɪk dɪˈziːz] 慢性病
  （chronically-ill patients 意为"慢性病患者"）
- cancer [ˈkænsəʳ] 癌症
- heart disease [hɑːt dɪˈziːz] 心脏病
- liver complaint [ˈlɪvəʳ kəmˈpleɪnt] 肝病
- malaria [məˈleəriə] 疟疾
- autism [ˈɔːtɪzəm] 自闭症
- melancholia [ˌmelənˈkəʊlɪə] 忧郁症

MP3-038

Politics

☑☑☑ 高频单词 Most frequently used vocabulary in the IELTS Test

publicity
[pʌ'blɪsɪ(ə)ti]

(n.) 宣传；公开场合

Nothing ruins an American presidential candidate's chances of election like some bad **publicity**.

reform
[rɪ'fɔːm]

(v.) 革新，改造

The government needs to **reform** our current immigration laws. It is currently too difficult for foreigners to immigrate to our country.

democratic
[ˌdemə'krætɪk]

(a.) 民主的

The election has been run according to **democratic** principles.

派 democracy [dɪ'mɒkrəsi] (n.) 民主（制度，政体，国家）

diversify
[daɪ'vɜːsɪ(ə)faɪ]

(v.) 使多样化

The government announced plans to **diversify** the economy over the next 5-10 years.

派 diverse [daɪ'vɜːs] (a.) 多样化的

参 various ['veəriəs] (a.) 各种的，多姿多彩的

assorted [ə'sɔːtɪd] (a.) 混杂的

miscellaneous [ˌmɪsə'leɪniəs] (a.) 混杂的

equality
[ɪ'kwɒlɪ(ə)ti]

(n.) 平等，同等

Equality for all people before the law is one of the necessities of a civilised society.

exploitation
[ˌeksplɔɪ'teɪʃən]

(n.) 剥削；开采

The **exploitation** of women and children by employers in developing countries is a serious issue.

MP3-039

parliament
[ˈpɑːləmənt]

(n.) 议会；**议院**；（大写）英国国会

The Prime Minister arrived at **parliament** house, only to be mobbed by the media waiting outside.

infrastructure
[ˈɪnfrəˌstrʌktʃəʳ]

(n.) **基础设施**（如：交通、水电、煤气的设置）

The telecommunications **infrastructure** in China is still being built.

politician
[ˌpɒlɪ(ə)ˈtɪʃən]

(n.) **政治家，政客**

Although **politicians** are voted in to act on behalf of the people, many are seen as criminals in nations with corrupt governments.

committee
[kəˈmɪti]

(n.) **委员会**

A new **committee** was set up to monitor the progress of the redevelopment project.

ministry
[ˈmɪnɪ(ə)stri]

(n.) **部门**；（政府的）**部**

The **Ministry** of Foreign Affairs was notified of the redevelopment project.

congress
[ˈkɒŋgres]

(n.) **国会**；（大写）**美国国会**

In the USA, the **congress** consists of two law-making bodies: the Senate and the House of Representatives.

autonomy
[ɔːˈtɒnəmi]

(n.) **自治（权）**

After a lot of internal conflict, East Timor was finally granted **autonomy** from Indonesia.

federal
[ˈfedərəl]

(a.) 联邦（制）的

Around the nation, voters are expected to choose a new president for the upcoming **federal** election.

imperial
[ɪmˈpɪəriəl]

(a.) 帝国的

The **imperial** power of the Roman Empire was responsible for the changes in law and culture in European history.

legislature
[ˈledʒɪ(ə)sleɪtʃəʳ]

(n.) 立法机关

New laws are often made and passed by a democratically elected **legislature**.

legislation
[ˌledʒɪ(ə)sˈleɪʃən]

(n.) 立法；**法律，法规**

New **legislation** is needed to govern some of the unforeseen consequences of the Internet.

election
[ɪˈlekʃən]

(n.) 选举

The **election** results will not be broadcast until this Saturday.

派 electioneering [ɪˌlekʃəˈnɪərɪŋ] (n.) 竞选活动，拉票活动

majority
[məˈdʒɒrɪ(ə)ti]

(n.) 大多数

The **majority** of the town's population voted against the re-election of the mayor.

minority
[maɪˈnɒrɪ(ə)ti]

(n.) 少数，少数民族

Refugees, although happy to escape their troubled nations, often find hardship as an ethnic **minority** in their new country.

MP3-040

liberty
[ˈlɪbəti]

(n.) 自由

The end of the French Revolution spelt a great new era of **liberty** and freedom.

liberation
[ˌlɪbəˈreɪʃən]

(n.) 解放；获得自由

The **liberation** of France in the Second World War led to the final demise of Nazi Germany.

conservative
[kənˈsɜːvətɪv]

(a.) 保守的；（大写）保守党的 (n.) 守旧人士；（大写）保守党员

Traditional styles and values are of higher importance than social change for **conservative** governments.

equitable
[ˈekwɪ(ə)təbəl]

(a.) 公平的，公正的

Laws of government are made to treat members of the public in an **equitable** way.

Labour Party
[ˈleɪbər ˈpɑːti]

(n.)〈英〉工党

The **Labour Party** in Britain has traditionally represented the beliefs and interests of the working class.

参 the ruling party 执政党
the opposition party 反对党

ban
[bæn]

(v.) 禁止，取缔 (n.) 禁令，禁止

After the spate of recent accidents from the use of firecrackers, the government has now **banned** its sale to minors.

enforce
[ɪnˈfɔːs]

(v.) 执行，实施（法律）

While governments are responsible for law-making, it is the job of the police to **enforce** it.

prohibit
[prə'hɪbɪ(ə)t]

(v.)（法律或社会规范）禁止

The government now **prohibits** the consumption of alcohol in public places.

nationalism
['næʃənəlɪzəm]

(n.) 民族主义，国家主义

Every four years, strong feelings of **nationalism** arise in people from around the world who are watching the Olympic Games.

forerunner
['fɔː,rʌnə^r]

(n.) 先驱

In America in the late 1960's, equal rights political leaders such as Martin Luther King were seen as the **forerunners** for future change.

dynastic
[daɪ'næstɪk]

(a.) 王朝的

Ancient Chinese history has an intriguing **dynastic** past.

collapse
[kə'læps]

(n.) (v.) 倒塌；崩溃，瓦解

The revolution led to the **collapse** of the existing government and the implementation of a new controlling party.

proclaim
[prə'kleɪm]

(v.) 公告，正式宣布

The government **proclaimed** that they would never give up in the fight against terrorism.

unity
['juːnɪ(ə)ti]

(n.) 一致；结合，联合

For the first time, all opposing political parties were in **unity** over the final decision.

MP3-041

revolutionary
[ˌrevəˈluːʃənəri]

(a.) 革命的；创新的

The recent **revolutionary** uprising has led to the demise of the existing conservative government.

派 revolution [ˌrevəˈluːʃən] (n.) 革命，变革
►the Industrial Revolution 工业革命

abandon
[əˈbændən]

(v.) 放弃；遗弃，离弃

With the recent conservative uprising in the political party, many members were forced to **abandon** their positions.

corruption
[kəˈrʌpʃən]

(n.) 贪污，腐败

The government organised a joint enquiry into allegations of **corruption** within the police force.

dictatorship
[dɪkˈteɪtəʃɪp]

(n.) 独裁政治

Dictatorships resulted in the suffering of its people.

negotiator
[nɪˈgəʊʃieɪtə^r]

(n.) 谈判者

A **negotiator** was brought in to ease the tension between the two sides.

派 negotiate [nɪˈgəʊʃieɪt] (v.) 谈判，协商
►negotiate with sb 与某人谈判
►negotiate for/about sth 谈判某事
negotiation [nɪˌgəʊʃiˈeɪʃən] (n.) 谈判，协商

violent
[ˈvaɪələnt]

(a.) 粗暴的；暴力的

The quiet demonstration soon turned into a **violent** protest.

intervention
[ˌɪntəˈvenʃən]

(n.) 介入，干预

Government **intervention** was required to monitor the agriculture industry.

☑☑☐ 精选单词 Specialised vocabulary used in the IELTS Test

Renaissance
[rɪˈneɪsəns]

(n.) 复兴，复苏；（大写）**文艺复兴** (a.) 文艺复兴时代的

Apart from heralding a burgeoning of art and culture, the **Renaissance** also gave rise to a rebirth in learning and free enquiry; all of which had a significant influence on the monarchs of the time.

endowment
[ɪnˈdaʊmənt]

(n.)（尤指对学校或医院的）**捐款**；天赋，天资

The school's **endowment** allows it to provide scholarships to students of low-income families.

debilitate
[dɪˈbɪlɪ(ə)teɪt]

(v.) **削弱**；使脆弱

The popularity of the future president was **debilitated** by the recent scandal.

sovereignty
[ˈsɒvrənti]

(n.) **主权，统治权**

The republican army would not stop fighting until they had complete **sovereignty** over their nation.

monarch
[ˈmɒnək]

(n.) **国王，元首**

Citizens of Denmark have a strong love for their **monarch**, Queen Margrethe II.

treaty
[ˈtriːti]

(n.) **条约**

Finally the conflict ended with the signing of a peace **treaty** by both sides.

MP3-042

embody
[ɪm'bɒdi]

(v.) 使具体化，具体呈现

The principles outlined in the leader's political speech **embodied** everything we were fighting for.

despotism
['despətɪzəm]

(n.)（统治者的）独裁，专制

The **despotism** of Julius Caesar in the Roman Empire was one of the most famous in history.

aristocratic
[ˌærɪ(ə)stə'krætɪk]

(a.) 贵族的

The forming of a parliament was a replacement for the much despised **aristocratic** rule of the past.

reverence
['revərəns]

(n.) 尊敬，崇敬

The speech contained deep **reverence** for the past president.

martial
['mɑːʃəl]

(a.) 军事的，战争的 martial ART 武术

After the country lifted **martial** law, the political rights of people increased.

搭 martial law 戒严法

prerogative
[prɪ'rɒgətɪv]

(n.) 特权

The mayor is the only city official with the **prerogative** to suspend business licenses.

egalitarian
[ɪˌgælɪ(ə)'teəriən]

(a.) 平等主义的 (n.) 平等主义者

venal
['viːnl]

(a.) 唯利是图的

plebeian
[plɪ'biːən]

(a.) 平民的；下层阶级的

inhabitant
[ɪn'hæbɪ(ə)tənt]

(n.) 居民

Australian culture, despite its British roots, is strongly **egalitarian**. Whereas the 'mother-country' still has a relatively strong class system borne of its **venal** past, the **plebeian** nature of Australia's early **inhabitants** (many of them poor convicts sent from England) has ensured Australia's evolution into a far more open and equal society.

nationhood
['neɪʃənhʊd]

(n.) 国家地位

sovereign
['sɒvrɪn]

(a.) 主权独立的 (n.) 元首，君主

constituency
[kən'stɪtʃuənsi]

(n.) 选区；选区中的全体选民

impose
[ɪm'pəʊz]

(v.) 强迫；麻烦别人做不愿做的事

Interestingly, this sense of equality has also become a part of Australian political life. Ever since it gained its **nationhood** and became a **sovereign** country in 1901, the Australian **constituency** has continued to bear a healthy disrespect for authority. Indeed, criticism of the rich, powerful and/or successful is almost considered a national duty. Australians resent those in power **imposing** their will upon the general public.

feminism
['femɪnɪzəm]

(n.) 女性主义

One more recent change in the Australian cultural and political landscape, meanwhile, has been the advent of **feminism**. Over the past 100 years, women have become increasingly assertive of their rights in all spheres of life. This has seen Australian women gain the right to vote and receive equal pay, among other things.

MP3-043

utopia
[juː'təʊpiə]

(n.) 乌托邦，理想国

destruction
[dɪ'strʌkʃən]

(n.) 破坏，毁灭，消灭

However, Australia is certainly no **utopia**. One of the more negative consequences of the country's disdain for the successful is known as the 'tall poppy syndrome'—as soon as someone excels at anything, thus becoming a tall poppy, the shorter poppies immediately set about cutting them down. This often results in the **destruction** of ambition and potential.

☑□□ 挑战单词 Sophisticated vocabulary used in the IELTS Test

tribesman
['traɪbzmən]

(n.) 部落成员

Control over the wealth generated from local agriculture was handed over to the chief **tribesman**.

Art · Entertainment · Sports · Leisure

☑☑☑ 高频单词 Most frequently used vocabulary in the IELTS Test

lifestyle
[ˈlaɪfstaɪl]

(n.) 生活方式

A relaxed **lifestyle** has been proven to result in longevity.

occasion
[əˈkeɪʒən]

(n.) 场合，时刻；重大活动

There are now an increasing number of events which young people can attend in order to celebrate various **occasions**.

exhibition
[ˌeksɪ(ə)ˈbɪʃən]

(n.) 展览

The **exhibition** will contain the works of many famous impressionist painters, including paintings by Monet.

搭 on exhibition 展览中
make an exhibition of oneself 当众出糗

同 display [dɪˈspleɪ] (n.) (v.) 陈列，展示

gallery
[ˈɡæləri]

(n.) 画廊，美术馆

The **gallery** aims to display a vast array of images from a variety of historical periods.

contemporary
[kənˈtempərəri]

(a.) 当代的，现代的

Contemporary art attempts to remove itself from religion, politics and other values in order to provide a purely aesthetic presentation of experience.

同 up-to-date [ˌʌptəˈdeɪt] (a.) 现代的，最新的
modern [ˈmɒdən] (a.) 现代的，时髦的

参 in order to = in an attempt to = with the intention to 为了…

MP3-045

aesthetic
[iːs'θetɪk]

(a.) 美学的；艺术的

Some artists argue that art should only be judged by its **aesthetic** value, that of its form, and not by its content.

impression
[ɪm'preʃən]

(n.) 印象

The play left a powerful and lasting **impression** on my mind.

派 impress [ɪm'pres] (v.) 使…印象深刻，使…钦佩
►be impressed by sth/sb 对…印象深刻
impressive [ɪm'presɪv] (a.) 令人赞叹的

cuisine
[kwɪ'ziːn]

(n.) 烹饪，料理；餐厅的高级菜肴

French **cuisine** is one of the country's most treasured possessions.

delicacy
['delɪkəsi]

(n.) 美食，佳肴

Snails, oysters and horsemeat are seen as **delicacies** in French cuisine.

派 delicate ['delɪkət] (a.)（物品）精致的，易碎的；（人）娇弱的

folksong
['fəʊksɒŋ]

(n.) 民谣

Traditional entertainment such as **folksongs** has been popular around the world since ancient times.

justifiable
['dʒʌstɪ(ə)faɪəbəl]

(a.) 有正当理由的

Dropping the worst player on the soccer team was **justifiable**.

artistic
[ɑː'tɪstɪk]

(a.) 艺术的；富有艺术创造力的

Only a handful of painters have shown true **artistic** talent in their artwork.

architect
[ˈɑːkɪ(ə)tekt]

(n.) 建筑师
An **architect** is employed in the preliminary stages of building a new house.

architecture
[ˈɑːkɪ(ə)tektʃəʳ]

(n.) 建筑物；建筑学
This particular church is a perfect example of eighteenth century **architecture**.

masterpiece
[ˈmɑːstəpiːs]

(n.) 杰作
The 'Mona Lisa' is Leonardo da Vinci's most popular **masterpiece**.

theatre
[ˈθɪətəʳ]

(n.) 戏院，剧场
In my free time I often go to the **theatre** to see the latest plays.

booth
[buːð]

(n.) 亭；（有篷的）货摊
Tickets can be obtained from the ticket **booth** around the corner.
搭 phone booth 公共电话亭
photo booth 自助式的快照间

performance
[pəˈfɔːməns]

(n.) 表演；表现
It was the most magnificent **performance** of Swan Lake I have ever seen.

audience
[ˈɔːdiəns]

(n.) 观众，听众
The **audience** was attracted by the delightful array of colours and other props on the stage.

MP3-046

spectator
[spekˈteɪtə^{r}]

(n.) 观众（尤指观看体育赛事的观众）

Several **spectators** of last night’s football game were arrested when a riot broke out in the upper tiers of the stadium.

fiction
[ˈfɪkʃən]

(n.) 小说；虚构的事

Fiction such as *The Lord of the Rings* has amazing creatures and warriors.

poetry
[ˈpəʊɪ(ə)tri]

(n.) 诗、诗歌的总称

Poetry about love has been used by people throughout history to convey their feelings.

参 poem [ˈpəʊɪm] (n.) （一首）诗

historian
[hɪˈstɔːriən]

(n.) 历史学家

Many **historians** have played an important role in detailing the demise of Nazi Germany.

literature
[ˈlɪtərətʃə^{r}]

(n.) 文学（作品）；文献；著述

Literature such as novels, plays and poems were more popular before TV was invented.

stimulus
[ˈstɪmjʊləs]

(n.) 刺激；促进因素

The large sign was used as a visual **stimulus** to get people’s attention.

perception
[pəˈsepʃən]

(n.) 感觉，知觉；理解

My **perception** of the meaning of the painting was completely wrong.

device
[dɪˈvaɪs]

(n.) 装置；计划；方法

A screen-printer is a **device** used to make artwork copies.

visual
[ˈvɪʒuəl]

(a.) **视觉的**

I have a strong **visual** memory of the horrific war movie.

critic
[ˈkrɪtɪk]

(n.) **评论家**

The movie **critic** wrote a great review of last night's film.

layout
[ˈleɪaʊt]

(n.) 安排；**设计**；陈设

The coach gave a brief description of the **layout** of the course.

vividness
[ˈvɪvɪdnəs]

(n.) **生动，逼真**；栩栩如生；鲜艳

The story of the boys' hardship was told with remarkable **vividness** throughout the movie.

派 vivid [ˈvɪvɪd] (a.) 鲜明的，生动的

episode
[ˈepɪ(ə)səʊd]

(n.) 插曲；**一段经历**；一集（电视剧）；一节（小说）

Training for the 2008 Olympics was one of the most difficult **episodes** of the sportstar's career.

calligraphy
[kəˈlɪgrəfi]

(n.) **书法**

Many Chinese practise **calligraphy** in their spare time.

leisure
[ˈleʒə]

(a.) **闲暇的，空闲的**

The younger generation prefers to have more **leisure** time to enjoy life than to work long hours.

country music
[ˈkʌntri ˈmjuːzɪk]

(n.) **乡村音乐**

Country music has become more mainstream in the last few years, thanks to a few country singers who have crossed over into the pop music scene.

MP3-047

musical
[ˈmjuːzɪkəl]

(n.) 音乐剧

Visitors to New York often venture to Broadway to take in a **musical**.

opera
[ˈɒpərə]

(n.) 歌剧

Even if they do not understand Italian, connoisseurs of **opera** still enjoy famous Italian **operas**.

sitcom
[ˈsɪtkɒm]

(n.) 情境喜剧（即 situation comedy）

I watch **sitcoms** to help myself unwind after a long day at the office.

immerse
[ɪˈmɜːs]

(v.) 使浸没；埋首于；完全投入于

The doctoral student **immersed** himself in his studies in order to obtain his PhD degree within three years.

sportsmanship
[ˈspɔːtsmənʃɪp]

(n.) 运动家精神

Sportsmanship can best be summed up in the phrase, ‘it is not whether you win or lose but how you play the game’.

hiking
[ˈhaɪkɪŋ]

(n.) 徒步行走，健行

Many people in Taiwan enjoy **hiking** since Taiwan possesses many spectacular mountain ranges.

championship
[ˈtʃæmpiənʃɪp]

(n.) 锦标赛，冠军赛

He won the **championship** by default as his top-rated opponent did not show up due to unforeseen circumstances.

gymnasium
[dʒɪmˈneɪziəm]

(n.) 体育馆；健身房（或作 gym）

The students entered the **gymnasium** to begin their physical education class.

parachute
[ˈpærəʃuːt]

(n.) 降落伞 (v.) 跳伞

I often wonder why commercial airlines equip their planes with life jackets but not with **parachutes**.

wrestling
[ˈreslɪŋ]

(n.) 摔跤

Greco-Roman **wrestling**, which is featured in the Olympics, is nothing like the professional **wrestling** we see on TV.

weightlifting
[ˈweɪtˌlɪftɪŋ]

(n.) 举重

After the accident, he took up **weightlifting** to help him regain his strength.

hilarious
[hɪˈleəriəs]

(a.) 有趣的，搞笑的

The characters in my favourite sitcom are so **hilarious** that each time I watch them I laugh my head off.

recreation
[ˌrekriˈeɪʃən]

(n.) 娱乐，消遣

The city council has set aside a lot of areas for **recreation**.

同 amusement [əˈmjuːzmənt] (n.) 娱乐，消遣活动
►amusement park 游乐园

relaxation
[ˌriːlækˈseɪʃən]

(n.) 松弛，放松身心

For **relaxation**, I take long walks around the neighbourhood.

pastime
[ˈpɑːstaɪm]

(n.) 消遣，娱乐

Bird watching is one of my favourite **pastimes**.

MP3-048

lyrics
[ˈlɪrɪks]

(n.) 歌词

I do not know the **lyrics** to the national anthem. Whenever I have to sing it, I just move my mouth and pretend I know them.

composer
[kəmˈpəuzəʳ]

(n.) 作曲家

Beethoven was one of the most skilled as well as the most unfortunate **composers**.

symphony
[ˈsɪmfəni]

(n.) 交响乐（团）

I finally got tickets to go and see the **symphony** perform Wagner.

handicraft
[ˈhændikrɑːft]

(n.) 手工艺（品）

I like to buy the local **handicrafts** when I go and visit another country.

sculpture
[ˈskʌlptʃəʳ]

(n.) 雕刻品；雕像

The **sculpture**, which is estimated to be worth more than £5 million, is to be auctioned at Sotheby's next month.

go cycling
[gəu ˈsaɪklɪŋ]

(v.) 骑自行车

If you plan to **go cycling** with us, you better buy a top-model bike as we go through some rough terrain.

☑☑☐ 精选单词 Specialised vocabulary used in the IELTS Test

metaphor
[ˈmetəfəʳ]

(n.) 隐喻，譬喻

Most poetry contains a vast number of **metaphors**, which are difficult to understand without explanation.

detrimental
[ˌdetrɪˈmentəl]

(a.) 有害的，不利的

Pop culture has had a **detrimental** effect on the areas of contemporary art and literature.

同 harmful [ˈhɑːmfəl] (a.) 有害的（尤指对健康或环境）
injurious [ɪnˈdʒʊəriəs] (a.) 造成伤害的，有害的

enlighten
[ɪnˈlaɪtn]

(v.) 启发，启蒙，教导

In order to **enlighten** the audience, the art critic explained the details of the painting.

masterful
[ˈmɑːstəfəl]

(a.) 技巧熟练的

The conductor was **masterful** in his performance with the national orchestra.

hearten
[ˈhɑːtn]

(v.) 使人快乐或振奋起来，大受鼓舞

The player's hopes were **heartened** after scoring the equaliser.

epic
[ˈepɪk]

(n.) 史诗（电影、文学作品等）

I'm in the mood to watch a good **epic** with lots of action and history.

saga
[ˈsɑːgə]

(n.) 传说；家族故事

The long story about the adventures and misfortunes of the family's life was a boring **saga**.

scenario
[sɪ(ə)ˈnɑːriəʊ]

(n.) 剧情，脚本；（行动的）方案；局面

A good football coach prepares his/her players for every possible **scenario**.

MP3-049

mythology
[mɪ'θɒlədʒi]

(n.) 神话（学）

Ancient Greek **mythology** tells stories of powerful gods and goddesses.

narrative
['nærətɪv]

(n.) 故事，叙述 (a.) 叙事的

The novel told a descriptive **narrative** of the hero's final journey.

Narrative fiction is my child's favourite style of Hollywood movie.

auspices
['ɔːspɪ(ə)sɪ(ə)z]

(n.) 支持，资助；主办

Under the **auspices** of their government, many athletes receive funding and special training.

angling
['æŋglɪŋ]

(n.) 垂钓

There are many **angling** programmes on TV which show you the best fishing spots and tips on how to make a catch.

ceramics
[sɪ(ə)'ræmɪks]

(n.) 陶制品；制陶艺术

She took up **ceramics** so she could learn how to make teacups to give to her friends for Christmas.

embroidery
[ɪm'brɔɪdəri]

(n.) 刺绣；刺绣品

Traditional Chinese **embroidery** techniques are famous the world over for their fine detail.

mountaineering
[ˌmaʊntɪ(ə)'nɪərɪŋ]

(n.) 登山运动

Mountaineering is more strenuous than hiking as mountaineers normally scale high peaks.

gusto
[ˈgʌstəʊ]

(n.) 兴致，享受，津津有味
I am usually not a big eater, but after playing football I eat with a lot of **gusto**.

rapt
[ræpt]

(a.) 专心投入的，全神贯注的
The audience was listening with **rapt** attention to the world-renowned pianist.

☑☐☐ 挑战单词 **Sophisticated vocabulary used in the IELTS Test**

philately
[fɪˈlætəli]

(n.) 集邮
Philately is a hobby which requires a considerable amount of time and money as a philatelist must generally acquire many stamps from around the world.

bent
[bent]

(n.) 天分，爱好 (a.) 弯曲的；下定决心的
My son oddly has a **bent** for fixing car engines despite the fact that he has never showed any aptitude for anything else mechanical.

■ 补充单词：各式运动

- volleyball [ˈvɒlibɔːl] 排球
- tennis [ˈtenɪs] 网球
- badminton [ˈbædmɪntən] 羽毛球
- boxing [ˈbɒksɪŋ] 拳击
- high jump [haɪ dʒʌmp] 跳高
- athletics [æθˈletɪks] 〈英〉田径运动（美式英语为 track and field）
- marathon [ˈmærəθən] 马拉松长跑

MP3-050

Business • Finance

☑☑☑ 高频单词 Most frequently used vocabulary in the IELTS Test

recruitment
[rɪˈkruːtmənt]

(n.) 招募新人

During the company's recent **recruitment** campaign, we were able to recruit graduates from some of the top universities in the UK.

resign
[rɪˈzaɪn]

(v.) 辞职

The vice president was pressured to **resign** after it became public that he had been involved in a corruption scandal.

firm
[fɜːm]

(n.)（规模较小的）公司

If you graduate from the top ten percent of Harvard Law School, you will have your pick of law **firms** to work at.

candidate
[ˈkændɪ(ə)dɪ(ə)t]

(n.) 候选人；求职者，应征者

Candidates for the new position of Marketing Manager will have to endure rigorous testing and a series of interviews before a decision will be made on whom to appoint.

executive
[ɪgˈzekjʊtɪv]

(a.) 行政的，执行的 (n.) 总经理，主管

The **executive** manager of the marketing department has an autocratic management style.

designation
[ˌdezɪgˈneɪʃən]

(n.) 指定，任命

The **designation** of a new General Manager pleased many of the staff who could not tolerate the last GM's authoritarian management style.

creditor
[ˈkredɪ(ə)təʳ]

(n.) 贷方，债权人

You better be careful and make the house mortgage repayment on time, otherwise you will have **creditors** chasing after you!

debtor
[ˈdetəʳ]

(n.) 借方，债务人

The bank uses the money that it receives from its investors to issue loans and increase the number of **debtors**.

profit and loss account
[ˈprɒfɪ(ə)t ənd lɒs əˈkaʊnt]

(n.)（企业）损益表

The balance on this company's **profit and loss account** is not good. If they don't increase their profits, they will soon go bankrupt.

profitable
[ˈprɒfɪtəbəl]

(a.) 有利润的；有益的

It's a very **profitable** organisation.

同 lucrative [ˈluːkrətɪv] (a.) 赚钱的

shareholder
[ˈʃeəˌhəʊldəʳ]

(n.)〈英〉股东

If you had been smart, you would have become a **shareholder** of Yahoo stock when the company first floated!

premium
[ˈpriːmiəm]

(n.) 酬金，奖金；额外的费用；保险费

This company doesn't give a **premium** with their stock shares because they choose to reinvest their profits back into the company.

My health insurance **premium** is $670 every month.

MP3-051

inventory
[ˈɪnvəntri]

(n.) 清单；〈美〉存货

I don't think we have OHPs (overhead projectors) on our **inventory** anymore.

advertising
[ˈædvətaɪzɪŋ]

(n.) **广告活动，广告宣传**

I know that our **advertising** expenses are high, but if we do not promote this product, nobody will buy it.

派 advertisement [ədˈvɜːtɪsmənt] (n.) 广告
►classified advertisements（报刊的）分类广告

commercial
[kəˈmɜːʃəl]

(n.)（电视或电台的）**商业广告** (a.) 商业的，买卖的

The **commercials** during the Olympics are all very interesting, but it must cost those companies a lot to air them.

franchise
[ˈfræntʃaɪz]

(v.) **授予经销权** (n.) 经销权

Our company would grow a lot if we **franchised**. However, we would have less control over each store.

market coverage
[ˈmɒːkɪ(ə)t ˈkʌvərɪdʒ]

(n.) **市场占有率**

Advertising through the newspaper has a **market coverage** of 65%.

point of sale
[pɔɪnt əv seɪl]

(n.) **产品销售点**

Point of sale advertising attracted many spontaneous purchases last month.

retail
[ˈriːteɪl]

(v.) **零售，通过商店或邮购销售**

That company's products are **retailing** well, but if they don't introduce any new products, they will soon fall behind the competition.

after-sales service
[ˈɒːftəʳ seɪls ˈsɜːvɪ(ə)s]

(n.) 售后服务

Refrigerators from this company may be very expensive, but they offer a lot of **after-sales service**.

penetrate
[ˈpenɪ(ə)treɪt]

(v.) 刺穿；进入，打入…市场；经过研究或调查而了解

Language and cultural barriers make the Chinese market very hard for Western companies to **penetrate**.

vending machine
[ˈvendɪŋ məˈʃiːn]

(n.) 自动贩卖机

Pepsi-Cola has the most **vending machines** on campus.

going-rate
[ˈgəʊɪŋ reɪt]

(n.) 市场价格；行情价；现行费率

The **going-rate** for most computers right now is much less than before.

prestige
[preˈstiːʒ]

(n.) 威信，声望 (a.) 有声望的

Sotheby's ability to get famous pieces of artwork to sell is based on its company's **prestige** as an auction house.

reputation
[ˌrepjʊˈteɪʃən]

(n.) 名誉，名声

The hotel has gained a good **reputation** for its service.

派 reputable [ˈrepjʊtəbəl] (a.) 名誉良好的，有信誉的

sponsorship
[ˈspɒnsəʃɪp]

(n.) 赞助；支持

Professional racers need to be funded by rich sponsors in order to have the money to race. Many companies consider this kind of **sponsorship** to be a good way of getting publicity.

派 sponsor [ˈspɒnsəʳ] (n.) 赞助商，捐款者 (v.) 赞助，举办，发起

MP3-052

distribution
[ˌdɪstrɪ(ə)ˈbjuːʃən]

(n.) 分派；分布；**货品供应**

The **distribution** channels for my company's products include small shops as well as department stores.

wholesale
[ˈhəʊlseɪl]

(adv.) **批发地；**成批地 (a.) 批发的；成批的 retail

You should consider buying your computer **wholesale**, as it is much cheaper that way.

consumption
[kənˈsʌmpʃən]

(n.) **消费；**消耗

Foreign investors are hoping that as the Chinese economy strengthens, **consumption** rates will increase.

revival
[rɪˈvaɪvəl]

(n.) **复苏；**再兴起；（经过一段长时间后）再上演

The investment by development firms into that blighted neighbourhood led to a **revival** of the entire area.

combat
[ˈkɒmbæt]

(v.) (n.) 战斗；**对抗**

The manager held a meeting with heads of departments to decide on what action could **combat** the widespread pilfering from their company. pilfer: 盗窃

同 battle [ˈbætəl] (v.) (n.) 斗争，战役
- ►win a battle but lose the war 因小失大

conflict [ˈkɒnflɪkt] (v.) (n.) 冲突，争论
- ►be in conflict 起冲突
- ►lead to armed conflict 引起武装冲突
- ►conflict with 与…抵触

boost
[buːst]

(n.) (v.) **推动，增进**

The opening of the production plant and the construction of the motorway will provide a major **boost** to the economy of the region.

globalise
[ˈgləʊbəlaɪz]

(v.) 使全球化

The increasing number of people who can speak English is another indicator of how much the world is **globalising**.

monetary
[ˈmʌnɪ(ə)təri]

(a.) 货币金融的；财政的

The International **Monetary** Fund is coming under increasing attack for its policies and their possible harmful effects on poor countries.

bankruptcy
[ˈbæŋkrʌptsi]

(n.) 破产；倒闭

That company was so big that when it was under threat of **bankruptcy**, the government gave it huge bail-out loans.

possessions
[pəˈzeʃənz]

(n.) 拥有物；财产

Advertising companies just want to convince you that the more **possessions** you have, the happier you will become.

poverty
[ˈpɒvəti]

(n.) 贫穷，贫困

Globalisation is said not to alleviate **poverty** as the profits multinational companies generate rarely remain in the third world where their manufacturing bases are located.

同 destitution [ˌdestɪ(ə)ˈtjuːʃən] (n.) 贫困，缺乏

wealthy
[ˈwelθi]

(a.) 富有的，富裕的

Oil profits from oil-producing countries such as Saudi Arabia, Iraq and Iran tend to make only a certain few businessmen **wealthy** rather than improve the wealth of the entire country.

派 wealth [welθ] (n.) 财富，富足

参 fortune [ˈfɔːtʃuːn] (n.) 巨款，财富；命运，机运

- ►make a fortune 赚大钱
- ►fortune teller 算命师

MP3-053

tycoon
[taɪ'kuːn]

(n.) 大亨，企业巨子

Donald Trump is perhaps the most famous real estate **tycoon** especially since the debut of his show 'The Apprentice'.

financial crisis
[fɪ(ə)'nænʃəl 'kraɪsɪ(ə)s]

(n.) 经济危机

The 1997 Asian **Financial Crisis** started when Thailand re-evaluated its currency.

lender
['lendəʳ]

(n.) 贷方

The **lender** of my college loans is my school's credit union.

swap
[swɒp]

(v.) 交换；以物易物

Unfortunately I cannot give you cash for this return, but I can **swap** it with a product of equal or lesser value.

currency
['kʌrənsi]

(n.) 货币

Because of the differences in the value of **currency**, goods in Europe are more expensive than in the United States.

stampede
[stæm'piːd]

(n.) 蜂拥；奔逃

Every time McDonald's offers a new toy with their Happy Meals, there is a **stampede** of mums taking their kids to the nearest store.

transaction
[træn'zækʃən]

(n.) 交易，买卖

I felt the **transaction** went very well but I think the guy I sold the car to might have thought it was still a little expensive.

commodity
[kə'mɒdɪ(ə)ti]

(n.) 物资，商品

Thailand is trying to boost its agricultural **commodities** that it has available for export.

appreciation
[əˌpriːʃi'eɪʃən]

(n.) 增值；感激

Real estate is a good investment because the **appreciation** value is often greater than other investments.

arrears
[ə'rɪəz]

(n.) 欠款，逾期债款

Their account had been in **arrears** ever since they bought their new house.

depression
[dɪ'preʃən]

(n.)（经济的）萧条；消沉，沮丧

The economic **depression** following the 1997 Asian Financial Crisis hit Hong Kong severely.

dividend
['dɪvɪ(ə)dənd]

(n.) 股息，红利；被除数

The **dividends** that I am getting from my stock in that company are quite good.

indebted
[ɪn'detɪ(ə)d]

(a.) 感恩的；负债的

The fast food chain was heavily **indebted** after the expansion into Asia did not go as planned.

inflation
[ɪn'fleɪʃən]

(n.) 通货膨胀

Because the rate of **inflation** is increasing so rapidly, the prices of goods fluctuate almost daily.

overdraft
['əʊvədrɑːft]

(n.) 透支款项

My bank account was overdrawn by an amount of $245. Because the **overdraft** was so large, I had to pay an additional fee to the bank.

MP3-054

depreciate
[dɪˈpriːʃieɪt]

(v.) 贬值；跌价

The value of my investments in the technology industry **depreciated** rapidly after the dot-com bubble burst.

overdue
[ˌəʊvəˈdjuː]

(a.) 过期未付的，逾期的

My electricity bill payment is two weeks **overdue**.

prosperity
[prɒˈsperɪ(ə)ti]

(n.) 成功，繁荣；发达

The **prosperity** of America's economy has had a positive effect on employment rates.

solvent
[ˈsɒlvənt]

(a.)（尤指公司，企业）有偿还能力的

The products that keep our business **solvent** are our best-selling Christmas ornaments.

outlay
[ˈaʊtleɪ]

(n.) 经费，开销

The aspiring entrepreneurs abandoned the new business plan as the large **outlays** involved made it too risky.

haggle
[ˈhægəl]

(v.) 议价，讨价还价　bargain.

I tried to **haggle** with him to get a lower price but I was unsuccessful.

sublet
[sʌbˈlet]

(v.) 转租，分租

I'm looking for somebody to **sublet** my apartment while I'm in London this summer vacation.

voucher
[ˈvaʊtʃəʳ]

(n.) 凭证；代券

When I returned my shoes to that store, I got a **voucher** that is good for buying another pair of shoes.

coupon
[ˈkuːpɒn]

(n.) 折价券

I know that I would be able to save a lot of money at the grocery store if I clipped **coupons**, but I find that too time-consuming.

consignment
[kənˈsaɪnmənt]

(n.) 托运的货物

The last **consignment** of goods still hasn't arrived. Could you please ask shipping to trace it?

freight
[freɪt]

(n.) 货运；货物；运费 (v.) 运输（货物）

The amount of goods that we move by **freight** every year has been increasing.

assurance
[əˈʃʊərəns]

(n.) 保证；确信；保险

Life **assurance** is essential especially when you are raising a family. You don't want your family in financial ruin if anything ever happens to you.

revenue
[ˈrevɪ(ə)njuː]

(n.) （公司或政府的）收入

Revenue less expenses equals profit.

discharge
[dɪsˈtʃɑːdʒ]

(v.) 出院；出狱；释出（不好的气体或液体）；履行

After she was **discharged** from the hospital, she went directly to her grandparents' house to recover.

subsidy
[ˈsʌbsɪ(ə)di]

(n.) 津贴，补助金

My company provides a **subsidy** for my transportation expenses to and from work.

joint venture
[dʒɔɪnt ˈventʃə[r]]

(n.) （两个公司以上的）企业合资

Toyota and Nissan are collaborating on a **joint venture** to develop a hydrogen-run vehicle.

MP3-055

perk
[pɜːk]

(n.) 津贴；福利 (v.) 使振奋

One of the **perks** of my job is that I get twenty paid vacation days after working a full year.

white-collar
[waɪt ˈkɒlə^{r}]

(a.) 白领阶层的

White-collar work may be less physically tiring than blue-collar work, but it tends to be more stressful.

drawback
[ˈdrɔːbæk]

(n.) 缺点

The only **drawback** of working at that company is that you have to work occasionally on Saturdays.

acumen
[ˈækjʊmən]

(n.) 正确敏锐的洞察力

Because of his **acumen**, we were able to avoid following through with a plan that would have been disastrous for our company.

autobiography
[ˌɔːtəbaɪˈɒgrəfi]

(n.) 自传

Sam Walton's **autobiography** gives some fascinating insights into his Wal-Mart empire.

subcontract
[ˌsʌbkənˈtrækt]

(v.) 转订契约；分包给…

I might suggest to the directors that some of this work should be **subcontracted** out.

seniority
[ˌsiːniˈɒrɪ(ə)ti]

(n.) 资深

I know that I should have pointed out the mistake in his business proposal, but because he has **seniority** over me, I was too afraid to.

anticipate
[æn'tɪsɪ(ə)peɪt]

(v.) **预期，期望；**在…之前行动

The company hadn't **anticipated** that so many people would attend the Grand Opening Sale and as a result there were scenes of chaos in front of the store involving frantic shoppers.

fluctuation
[ˌflʌktʃʊ'eɪʃən]

(n.)（尤指价格、汇率及气候上的）**波动、起伏或变化**

The recent **fluctuations** in the stock market have made all the investors nervous.

counteract
[ˌkaʊntər'ækt]

(v.) **减轻，消除**（不好的事物的影响）

The only way to **counteract** the negative effects of the recent economic downturn is to lower our prices.

speculation
[ˌspekjʊ'leɪʃən]

(n.) **投机**（买卖生意）；臆测

Speculation by foreign investors into the South-East Asian markets is partly to blame for the 1997 Asian Financial Crisis.

capacity
[kə'pæsɪ(ə)ti]

(n.) 容量；**生产力；**能力；职务

Our factory is currently running under **capacity** because orders have been lower than usual this summer.

flexibility
[ˌfleksɪ(ə)'bɪlɪ(ə)ti]

(n.) **弹性，适应性，**变通

This job requires me to have a lot of **flexibility** because there are always new things coming up.

norm
[nɔːm]

(n.) **标准，常态；**规范

It has often been mentioned that if you want to do business in developing countries, slush funds are necessary as bribes are the **norm**.

MP3-056

☑☑☐ 精选单词 Specialised vocabulary used in the IELTS Test

fictitious transaction
[fɪkˈtɪʃəs trænˈzækʃən]

(n.) 买空卖空

It was alleged that he had executed **fictitious transactions**. A show cause notice was issued accordingly.

endowment
[ɪnˈdaʊmənt]

(n.) 捐款；天资，天分

The main reason that that particular non-profit organisation is able to run is because of a large **endowment** from Aerie Corporation.

surplus value
[ˈsɜːpləs ˈvæljuː]

(n.) 剩余价值

The **surplus value** left from these products will allow us to provide greater benefits for our employees.

indemnity
[ɪnˈdemnɪ(ə)ti]

(n.) 赔偿；保障

She was quite distraught after learning that her professional **indemnity** insurance did not cover the damages caused in the workplace accident.

penury
[ˈpenjʊri]

(n.) 赤贫，穷困

Many peasant families in Bangladesh live their life in **penury**.

token
[ˈtəʊkən]

(n.) 象征；（机器用的）代币；〈英〉现金礼券

As a **token** of our appreciation, please accept this present for all your hard work.

practitioner
[prækˈtɪʃənə^{r}]

(n.) 专业人士，开业者（尤指律师、医生）

GP is short for general **practitioner**. In countries like Australia you need to get a referral from one if you want to see a specialist.

thrifty
[ˈθrɪfti]

(a.) 节俭的

He is very **thrifty**, by that I mean he is always looking for ways to save money.

shortfall
[ˈʃɔːtfɔːl]

(n.) 欠缺之处；不足（额）

The company will have to take measures immediately to cover the massive **shortfall** incurred last quarter.

stipend
[ˈstaɪpend]

(n.) 固定津贴

The monthly **stipend** she receives from the school's research department is just enough to pay her expenses.

honorarium
[ˌɒnəˈreəriəm]

(n.)（指金额较小的）谢礼，酬金

I received an **honorarium** of $100 for editing an article for that newspaper.

blue-collar
[bluː ˈkɒlə[r]]

(a.) 蓝领阶层的，体力劳动的

A hundred years ago a **blue-collar** job would have been sufficient to provide for the entire family. These days it's becoming increasingly more difficult.

☑☐☐ 挑战单词 Sophisticated vocabulary used in the IELTS Test

amenable
[əˈmiːnəbəl]

(a.) 愿意接受或改变的；适合…情况的

If you are not **amenable** to complete this project, I will have to find somebody else to replace you.

upkeep
[ˈʌpkiːp]

(n.) 生活费；维护、保养费

The household's **upkeep** costs increased after the birth of their first child.

Theme 9

MP3-057

Work

☑☑☑ 高频单词 Most frequently used vocabulary in the IELTS Test

routine
[ruː'tiːn]

(n.) 例行公事；**惯例** (a.) 例行的，日常的

In some countries, going to the pub for a drink after work is part of one's daily **routine**.

redundant
[rɪ'dʌndənt]

(a.)〈英〉**因人员过剩而被解雇的**；多余的

The company could no longer afford to keep so many employees so some had to be made **redundant**.

confidential
[ˌkɒnfɪ(ə)'denʃəl]

(a.) **机密的**

The **confidential** documents on the worsening state of the company's finances were somehow leaked to the media.

promotion
[prə'məʊʃən]

(n.) **升迁**；宣传（活动）

It's becoming increasingly important to have at least a Master's Degree in order to gain a **promotion** in a company.

probation
[prə'beɪʃən]

(n.) **试用（期）**；缓刑（期）

The first three months of your employment will be the **probation** period, during which you will not be eligible for vacation leave.

unemployment
[ˌʌnɪm'plɔɪmənt]

(n.) **失业（人数，状态）**

The last recovery of the American economy is being called a 'jobless recovery'. This is because productivity has increased but **unemployment** still remains a problem.

派 employ [ɪm'plɔɪ] (v.) 雇用
►be employed in doing sth 忙于…
employee [ɪm'plɔiː] (n.) 受雇者，员工
employer [ɪm'plɔɪə^r] (n.) 雇主，老板

competition
[ˌkɒmpɪ(ə)ˈtɪʃən]

(n.) 比赛；**竞争（者）**
The **competition** from new companies entering the market has forced our company to cut costs.

workaholic
[ˌwɜːkəˈhɒlɪk]

(n.)〈常贬〉**工作狂**
She is such a **workaholic**. If she had a bed in her office, I'm sure she'd live there.

incentive
[ɪnˈsentɪv]

(n.) 刺激；**动力，诱因**
The new position opening in the marketing department has been my **incentive** to work so hard.

demanding
[dɪˈmɑːndɪŋ]

(a.) **极费心力的；**过分要求的
If only this job were less **demanding**, I would be able to spend more time with my family.

freelance
[ˈfriːlɑːns]

(a.) **自由职业的** (n.) 自由作家、记者、演员等 (v.) 从事自由职业
Because journalism is a hard field to get into for young graduates, he first had to do **freelance** writing.

manufacturing
[ˌmænjʊˈfæktʃərɪŋ]

(a.) **制造业的** (n.) 制造（业）
More and more **manufacturing** jobs are moving from developed countries to developing countries.

contribution
[ˌkɒntrɪ(ə)ˈbjuːʃən]

(n.) **贡献；**捐款；分摊额
This presentation would not have been possible without the **contributions** from my fellow coworkers.

potential
[pəˈtenʃəl]

(n.) **潜力，潜能** (a.) 潜在的，有潜力的，有可能的
Even though this employee is young, I believe he has the **potential** to become a manager in this company.

MP3-058

consumer
[kən'sjuːmər]

(n.) 消费者，顾客

The government is hoping that **consumer** spending will increase if they lower interest rates.

retailer
['riːteɪlər]

(n.) 零售商

The biggest clothing **retailer** has stores not only in our city, but also throughout the country.

involve
[ɪn'vɒlv]

(v.) 涉足；卷入；包含；需要

She's been **involved** with the Unions for many years, much to the dissatisfaction of her employer.

night shift
[naɪt ʃɪft]

(n.) 夜班

I have no idea why anyone would want to work the **night shift** if the pay is no higher than the day shift.

profession
[prə'feʃən]

(n.) 职业；专业；声明

If you want to enter the medical **profession**, you will have to study harder.

同 occupation [ˌɒkjʊ'peɪʃən] (n.) 工作；占领，占用
►occupational hazard 职业病，职业伤害
vocation [və'keɪʃən] (n.) 职业（尤指自认擅长且富使命感的工作）
►vocational education 职业教育
employment [ɪm'plɔɪmənt] (n.) 工作（着重在赚钱维生的层面），受雇，就业

target client
['tɑːgɪ(ə)t 'klaɪənt]

(n.) 目标顾客，目标客户

We want to have commercials during that show because its audience is the same age and gender as our **target clients**.

dismiss
[dɪs'mɪs]

(v.) 解雇，解散，遣散；剔除

I was **dismissed** from this task force as I no longer had the time to fulfil my duties properly.

warehouse
[ˈweəhaʊs]

(n.)（尤指储存待售货品的）仓库

Our in-store inventory is getting low. We'll have to get some more boxes from the **warehouse**.

assemble
[əˈsembəl]

(v.) 集合，聚集；装配，组合

Most car factories in the UK **assemble** cars out of parts that are made in other countries.

expand
[ɪkˈspænd]

(v.) 扩张；增加

The Chinese have to earn more money before its consumer market can **expand**.

thriving
[ˈθraɪvɪŋ]

(a.) 欣欣向荣的，成长的

New college graduates are able to easily find jobs because the economy is **thriving**.

派 thrive [θraɪv] (v.) 繁荣，蓬勃发展
参 flourish [ˈflʌrɪʃ] (v.) 繁荣，兴旺
prosper [ˈprɒspəʳ] (v.) 繁荣，发达

tax cut
[tæks kʌt]

(n.) 减税

Tax cuts are such a complicated issue because everyone wants to pay less taxes. Moreover, if we pay less taxes, we get fewer services from the government.

turnover
[ˈtɜːnəʊvəʳ]

(n.) 成交量；营业额，收入

The company **turnover** has been on the decrease for almost a year now and as a result workers may be made redundant or have their salaries cut.

同 revenue [ˈrevənjuː] (n.) 收入

overheads
[ˈəʊvəhedz]

(n.)（公司）必要开销（如水电费、房租）

Overheads like water and electricity increase the price of factories' products a lot.

MP3-059

recession
[rɪ'seʃən]

(n.) 经济衰退（期）

Some countries never fully recovered from the **recession** experienced in the days of the Asian Financial Crisis.

dramatically
[drə'mætɪkli]

(adv.) 戏剧（性）地，不寻常地；**突然且巨大地**

Our revenues from our mobile phone product lines increased **dramatically** after we entered the China market.

loss
[lɒs]

(n.) 遗失，失去；**损失**

The retirement of their CEO was a major **loss** for that company.

representative
[ˌreprɪ(ə)'zentətɪv]

(n.) **代表**

Our company's **representatives** in the Middle East can all speak Arabic.

reliability
[rɪˌlaɪə'bɪlɪ(ə)ti]

(n.) **可靠，可信赖**

Although they have great after service, the **reliability** of their products leaves a lot to be desired.

up-to-date
[ʌp tə deɪt]

(a.) **最新的**

The most **up-to-date** news about the financial markets is that they are improving.

compensation
[ˌkɒmpən'seɪʃən]

(n.) **赔偿，补偿**

The amount of **compensation** that companies are giving to customers who sue them is getting less and less.

The **compensation** package they gave him after he was laid off included a full month's pay.

MBA-holder
[ˌembiːˈeɪ ˈhəʊldəʳ]

(n.) 拥有 MBA学位者

The economy is getting so bad that even **MBA-holders** are struggling to find jobs.

recruiter
[rɪˈkruːtəʳ]

(n.) 负责招募工作的人员

Our **recruiters** are trained to not only consider an applicant's academic and professional record, but also certain 'personality' traits such as confidence and work ethic.

paycheque
[ˈpeɪtʃek]

(n.) 工资，薪资；支付薪资的支票

Paycheques come fortnightly at our company. If you need money sooner, you must contact the human resources office.

criteria
[kraɪˈtɪəriə]

(n.) 依据，标准（单数为 criterion）

We use several **criteria** when considering a recruit for a position in our company, including educational background and professional experience.

internship
[ˈɪntɜːnʃɪp]

(n.) 实习（期）

The **internship** I completed in my junior year of college was a very valuable learning experience.

layoff
[ˈleɪɒf]

(n.) 解雇（动词词组为 lay off）

After the most recent round of **layoffs**, our labour costs have stabilised.

After he was **laid off** from the factory, he had a hard time finding another job.

MP3-060

retain
[rɪ'teɪn]

(v.) 保留；保持

They are trying to **retain** as many employees after the merger as possible.

suspend
[sə'spend]

(v.) 暂时中止；暂缓，悬吊

The government decided to **suspend** the Defence Minister from his duties until the political prisoner crisis blew over.

expenditure
[ɪk'spendɪtʃə^r]

(n.) 经费，开销

If we don't cut our **expenditures** very soon, we will become bankrupt.

participate
[pɑː'tɪsɪ(ə)peɪt]

(v.) 参加，参与

In order to get as many people to **participate** in our focus group as possible, we are offering free lunch as well as $50.

insufficient
[ˌɪnsə'fɪʃənt]

(a.) 不足的

The work that you are putting into this project is **insufficient**. You'll need to cut your responsibilities in other areas so that you can pay more attention to this project.

☑☑□ 精选单词 Specialised vocabulary used in the IELTS Test

increment
['ɪŋkrɪ(ə)mənt]

(n.)（连续的，累积的）增额；增加

By law, employers must give their staff annual pay **increments**.

bond broker
[bɒnd 'brəʊkə^r]

(n.) 证券经纪人

I like to go to Mr Smith to buy my bonds because he charges less than other **bond brokers**.

direct boss
[dɪ(ə)ˈrekt bɒs]

(n.) 直属上司

My **direct boss** is often out of the office so I'm also accountable to the GM (General Manager).

public expenditure
[ˈpʌblɪk ɪkˈspendɪtʃə^{r}]

(n.) 公用开支

Because of the budget deficit, the government will have to cut its **public expenditure**.

product line
[ˈprɒdʌkt laɪn]

(n.) 生产线

Most of our shoes are only worn by old ladies with sore feet. We should introduce a new **product line** that specialises in shoes for teenagers.

mass-produced
[mæs prəˈdjuːst]

(a.) 大量生产的

The first **mass-produced** automobile was the Model-T. All other cars before the Model-T were assembled by hand.

rescind
[rɪˈsɪnd]

(v.) 撤回；废除；宣告…无效

We must **rescind** this policy as it is causing much dissatisfaction among our employees.

MP3-061

Media • Communication

☑☑☑ 高频单词 Most frequently used vocabulary in the IELTS Test

tabloid
[ˈtæblɔɪd]

(n.)（八卦）小报
The news of the famous couple's wedding hit the **tabloids** the very next day.

periodical
[ˌpɪəriˈɒdɪkəl]

(n.) 期刊，杂志
The science **periodical** keeps me up-to-date on advances every month.

invasion
[ɪnˈveɪʒən]

(n.) 入侵，侵犯
The paparazzi are always an **invasion** of famous actors' privacy.

censorship
[ˈsensəʃɪp]

(n.)（针对报刊、电影、电视节目的）审查制度
The magazine followed the rules of **censorship** in publishing the explicit photos.

libel
[ˈlaɪbəl]

(n.) 诽谤（文） (v.) 以文字诽谤
The UK has some of the strictest **libel** action in the world.

paparazzi
[ˌpæpəˈrætsi]

(n.) 狗仔队
Photos taken by the **paparazzi** are always published in gossip magazines.

journalism
[ˈdʒɜːnəlɪzəm]

(n.) 新闻杂志业；新闻学
The art of professional **journalism** was something the young writer needed to learn.

journalist
[ˈdʒɜːnəlɪst]

(n.) 新闻从业人员

Journalists cover important events occurring all around the world.

accusation
[ˌækjʊˈzeɪʃən]

(n.) 指控；举发

Serious **accusations** were made against the media, namely the paparazzi, as they were seen to be a major contributing factor in the death of Princess Diana.

documentary
[ˌdɒkjʊˈmentərɪ]

(n.) 纪录片

Nature **documentaries** are filmed in jungles all over Africa.

correspondence
[ˌkɒrɪˈspɒndəns]

(n.) 符合；通信；书信

Personal **correspondence** in the form of letters was popular for soldiers in the war.

columnist
[ˈkɒləmnɪst]

(n.) 专栏作家

She was the best **columnist** the newspaper had ever had.

broadcast
[ˈbrɔːdkaːst]

(v.) 广播，转播；散布 (n.) 广播（节目），电视转播

Important national news stories are often **broadcast** worldwide.

commercial
[kəˈmɜːʃəl]

(n.)（商业）广告

Television **commercials** are an effective way to advertise.

telecommunications
[ˌtelikəmjuːnɪ(ə)ˈkeɪʃənz]

(n.) 电信

The world has become smaller due to advances in **telecommunications** around the world.

MP3-062

headline
[ˈhedlaɪn]

(n.) 头版头条；标题；新闻提要

The newspaper **headline** told the world of the president's death.

critic
[ˈkrɪtɪk]

(n.)（尤指文学、艺术）评论家

The **critic** from the *New York Times* wrote a favourable review of the play.

satellite
[ˈsætɪ(ə)laɪt]

(n.) 人造卫星

Satellites now enable the world to watch the news as it happens.

drama series
[ˈdrɑːmə ˈsɪəriːz]

(n.) 连续剧

The TV **drama series** continued every Monday night with surprising twists in the story.

soap opera
[səʊp ˈɒpərə]

(n.) 电视肥皂剧

Australian **soap operas** such as 'Neighbours' are very popular in the UK.

current affairs
[ˈkʌrənt əˈfeəʳz]

(n.) 时事

We learned about the recent news from the **current affairs** programme.

laptop
[ˈlæptɒp]

(n.) 手提电脑

I can now use my new **laptop** computer at home as well as the office.

参 desktop [ˈdesktɒp] (n.) 台式计算机

communicative
[kəˈmjuːnɪ(ə)kətɪv]

(a.) 沟通的；健谈的，爱说话的

There has been renewed interest in **communicative** methods of English language teaching.

expressive
[ɪk'spresɪv]

(a.) 表情丰富的；**意味深长的**

The newspaper article was written in a very **expressive** style.

explanatory
[ɪk'splænətəri]

(a.) **解释的，说明的**

Explanatory measures were needed in order to make the new recruits understand.

conclusive
[kən'kluːsɪv]

(a.) 结论性的；**毋庸置疑的**

Throughout the trial, the evidence was **conclusive**. He was definitely guilty.

interactive
[ˌɪntər'æktɪv]

(a.) 互相作用的；**互动的**

In order to have an **interactive** meeting, everyone has to present their opinion.

commentator
['kɒmənteɪtə[r]]

(n.) **广播评论员，实况播报员**

While reporting the soccer final, the sports **commentator** got overexcited.

specific
[spɪ(ə)'sɪfɪk]

(a.) **明确的，确切的**

Specific information about the victims of the accident was not released by the authorities.

linguist
['lɪŋgwɪ(ə)st]

(n.) **精通多种外语的人**；语言学家

Due to a lot of travelling, foreign correspondents are great **linguists**.

参 bilingual [baɪ'lɪŋgwəl] (a.) 双语的，会说两种语言的

descriptive
[dɪ'skrɪptɪv]

(a.)（详细、有趣地）**描述的，说明的**

Some novels are so **descriptive** that you feel like you are there.

MP3-063

publication
[ˌpʌblɪ(ə)ˈkeɪʃən]

(n.) 出版（品）；刊物

The newspaper editor decided to stop the **publication** of the offensive pictures.

comic
[ˈkɒmɪk]

(n.) 漫画（书）；喜剧演员

Superhero **comics** are the best form of relaxation reading.

misinterpret
[ˌmɪsɪnˈtɜːprɪ(ə)t]

(v.) 曲解；误译

It is easy to **misinterpret** what someone from another culture is saying.

dispute
[dɪˈspjuːt]

(n.)(v.) 争论，辩论

After the successful meeting, the **dispute** was resolved.

派 disputatious [ˌdispjʊˈteɪʃəs] (a.) 好辩的，争议性的（正式用语）
indisputable [ˌɪndɪˈspjuːtəbəl] (a.) 毋庸置疑的
indisputably = without dispute = undoubtedly 毋庸置疑地

同 controversy [ˈkɒntrəvɜːsi] (n.)（公开的）争论，争辩
argument [ˈɑːgjʊmənt] (n.) 争论，论点

coax
[kəʊks]

(v.) 哄；用好话劝说

The fireman **coaxed** the frightened cat to come down from the tree.

abrupt
[əˈbrʌpt]

(a.) 突然的，不在预期之内的；不友善的

The meeting came to an **abrupt** end when the fire alarm rang.

defame
[dɪˈfeɪm]

(v.) 诽谤，中伤

If you **defame** someone, he can take you to court.

acquaint
[ə'kweɪnt]

(v.) 使…了解；告知

Life will be much easier for you in this country once you **acquaint** yourself with the 'laws of the land'.

派 acquainted [ə'kweɪntɪd] (a.) 熟悉的，了解的
▶be acquainted with sb/sth 熟悉…
acquaintance [ə'kweɪntəns] (n.) 认识但不是很熟的人，泛泛之交
▶first acquaintance with sb/sth 初次见面，初次接触
▶make the acquaintance with sb 与某人结识

premise
['premɪ(ə)s]

(n.) 前提；根据

There is no use arguing against you because even the **premise** of your argument is faulty.

profess
[prə'fes]

(v.) 佯称，声称

I cannot **profess** to believe things that are simply implausible.

refute
[rɪ'fjuːt]

(v.) 驳斥，反驳

I categorically **refute** your argument.

☑☑☐ 精选单词 Specialised vocabulary used in the IELTS Test

newsprint
['njuːzˌprɪnt]

(n.) 新闻用纸

Newspapers have used **newsprint** to print the news on for many years.

newsstand
['njuːzstænd]

(n.) 报摊

Every day I like to buy the newspaper from the local **newsstand**.

MP3-064

medium
[ˈmiːdiəm]

(n.) 媒介；**媒体；**表达思想的工具、手段

Television is the most popular **medium** to receive the daily news around the world.

mass media
[ˌmæs ˈmiːdiə]

(n.) **大众传播媒体**

News of the destruction in Iraq hit the **mass media** around the world.

circulation
[ˌsɜːkjʊˈleɪʃən]

(n.) **流通；**发行量；循环；销路

The **circulation** of the magazine was withdrawn due to its explicit content.

newsreel
[ˈnjuːzriːl]

(n.) **新闻（纪实）影片**

Newsreel footage of the final stages of WWII has now been transferred to colour.

squabble
[ˈskwɒbəl]

(v.)（为了小事）**争辩，口角**

The family continually **squabbled** over who would clean the dishes every night.

pent-up
[ˌpent ˈʌp]

(a.)（情绪）**被抑制的，无法发泄的**

The punching bag allowed him to release **pent-up** aggression.

decipher
[dɪˈsaɪfəʳ]

(v.) **辨读；**解码；翻译（尤指难以辨认的）

The enemy army were able to **decipher** what the code meant.

paradox
[ˈpærədɒks]

(n.) **自相矛盾的论调、事物、现象**

It's a **paradox** that the media fabricate stories when their aim should be to learn the truth.

expound
[ɪk'spaʊnd]

(v.) 阐述；详细解释

The more the professor **expounded** upon the theory, the more the students became confused.

notion
['nəʊʃən]

(n.) 概念，观念，想法

The **notion** that technology has made our lives easier is not entirely true; in some respects it has made life more complex.

wheedle
['wiːdl]

(v.) 以谄媚的方式或甜言蜜语来诱惑他人以获得自己想要的事物

I had to **wheedle** the information out of him.

slander
['slɑːndə^r]

(v.) (n.) 诽谤，诋毁中伤

After Barry's name was **slandered** in the press, he stood no chance of winning the election.

affable
['æfəbəl]

(a.) 友善且容易交谈的

At first I thought he was standoffish, but after getting to know him, I find him to be a very **affable** person.

☑☐☐ 挑战单词 Sophisticated vocabulary used in the IELTS Test

promulgate
['prɒməlgeɪt]

(v.) 发布，传播

The ideas were soon **promulgated** by the chairman to everyone at the meeting.

anecdotal
[ˌænɪk'dəʊtl]

(a.) 轶事的，趣闻的

Details of the criminal's elaborate story were seen in court as only **anecdotal** evidence.

MP3-065

commune
[kə'mjuːn]

(v.) 与…亲密交谈；**与…亲近**

I like to **commune** with nature, so I often go to the park early in the morning and take walks.

ignominy
['ɪgnəmɪni]

(n.) **耻辱；**公众的羞辱

He suffered great **ignominy** after news of his affair was made public.

loquacious
[ləʊ'kweɪʃəs]

(a.) 话多的；**滔滔不绝的**

Her **loquacious** lawyer would spend hours talking to the media about her case if she allowed him.

同 garrulous ['gærələs] (a.) 喋喋不休的，碎念的
talkative ['tɔːkətɪv] (a.) 爱说话的，健谈的

platitude
['plætɪ(ə)tjuːd]

(n.) **陈腔滥调；**单调

That book is full of **platitudes** and does not say anything not heard of before.

MP3-066

Education • Study

☑☑☑ 高频单词 Most frequently used vocabulary in the IELTS Test

literacy
[ˈlɪtərəsi]

(n.) 识字，会读会写；特殊领域的专业知识

The government is seeking to increase the **literacy** rate from 93% to 95% in the next 5 years.

派 literate [ˈlɪtərət] (a.) 识字的，有文化的
illiterate [ɪˈlɪtərət] (a.) 文盲的 (n.) 文盲

correspondence
[ˌkɒrɪ(ə)ˈspɒndəns]

(n.) 通信；符合，一致；函授

Learning through **correspondence** has increased in popularity during the last decade.

distance learning
[ˈdɪstəns ˈlɜːnɪŋ]

(n.) 远距教学

More and more tertiary institutions are offering **distance learning** courses for their students.

dissertation
[ˌdɪsəˈteɪʃən]

(n.) 专题论文，学位论文

In order to complete her PhD, she needs to submit her 100,000 word **dissertation** by the end of the semester.

satisfactory
[ˌsætɪ(ə)sˈfæktəri]

(a.) 令人满意的；符合要求的

Due to the thirst for knowledge, the need for a **satisfactory** education is greater than ever before in China.

reputable
[ˈrepjʊtəbəl]

(a.) 声誉高的，有声望的

It's nearly impossible to get a decent job without a qualification from a **reputable** institution.

MP3-067

perceive
[pə′siːv]

(v.) 察觉，意识到；领悟

The lecturer **perceived** amongst his students a lack of interest in the course.

perception
[pə′sepʃən]

(n.) 想法，看法；洞察力

The public **perception** of how the Ministry of Education handled the crisis was not very favourable.

comprehensive
[ˌkɒmprɪ′hensiv]

(a.) 广泛的；全面的；具理解能力的

The value of a **comprehensive** education can't be overstated.

ramifications
[ˌræmɪ(ə)fɪ(ə)′keɪʃənz]

(n.) 后果；分枝；分叉

The vice-chancellor's decision has had serious **ramifications** for the university.

undertake
[ˌʌndə′teɪk]

(v.) 着手进行；允诺，保证；接受

We had to **undertake** a major research project during our senior year.

tutorial
[tjuː′tɔːriəl]

(n.)（个人或小组的）指导老师的课后辅导

Tutorials are an essential component of tertiary education.

submit
[səb′mɪt]

(v.) 屈服，顺从；提交

All PhD students need to **submit** a thesis in order to complete their doctorate.

submission
[səb′mɪʃən]

(n.) 顺从；提交

The **submission** date of the politics assignment is no later than May 29th.

descriptive
[dɪˈskrɪptɪv]

(a.) **描述性的，陈述的**

Writing Task I in the IELTS academic module is a **descriptive** essay. Be sure to only describe the facts and not speculate.

intellectual
[ˌɪntɪ(ə)ˈlektʃʊəl]

(a.) **需用智力的，理解力强的** (n.) 知识分子

The phenomenon of globalisation has resulted in fierce **intellectual** debate in many academic circles.

controversy
[kɒnˈtrəvɜːsi]

(n.) **争议，争论；** 辩论

These days corporal punishment in schools causes much more **controversy** than it did in the past.

hypothetical
[ˌhaɪpəˈθetɪkəl]

(a.) **假设的；** 臆测的

Hypothetical situations are often far removed from real-life ones.

indefinite
[ɪnˈdefənɪ(ə)t]

(a.) 不明确的；**无确切（时间）限制的**

The completion date for his studies remains **indefinite**.

discriminate
[dɪˈskrɪmɪ(ə)neɪt]

(v.) **分辨，区别；** 歧视，差别对待

A successful student needs to **discriminate** between relevant and irrelevant information.

perspective
[pəˈspektɪv]

(n.) **想法，观点；** 远景；透视图法

The outspoken professor doesn't share the same **perspective** as his peers.

inquisitive
[ɪnˈkwɪzɪ(ə)tɪv]

(a.)〈贬〉过分好问的，爱打听的；**追根究底的**

An **inquisitive** mind is a prerequisite for scientific advancement.

MP3-068

experimental
[ɪkˌsperɪ(ə)ˈmentl]

(a.) 实验的

The university will build a state-of-the-art **experimental** centre that hopes to put the chemistry department at the leading edge of research.

comparison
[kəmˈpærɪ(ə)sən]

(n.) 比较，对照

In **comparison** to developing countries, advanced nations have much higher literacy rates.

搭 in comparison to 与…相较

radical
[ˈrædɪkəl]

(a.) 完全的，彻底的；激进的

The current government is proposing **radical** changes to the education system.

precisely
[prɪˈsaɪsli]

(adv.) 准确地；精确地；〈口〉的确没错

Precisely 22,355 students are enrolled at the University of Reading.

substantially
[səbˈstænʃəli]

(adv.) 可观地；大致上地

The number of full-time students enrolled at university has risen **substantially** in the last decade.

pupil
[ˈpjuːpəl]

(n.) 学生，学员（尤指小学生）

The **pupils** in her painting class are all six to seven years old.

truant
[ˈtruːənt]

(n.) 逃学生，旷课生

Children who come from broken families are more likely to play **truant**.

搭 play truant 旷课，逃学

acquisition
[ˌækwɪ(ə)ˈzɪʃən]

(n.) **获得，习得**
The language **acquisition** rate of younger children is much faster than adults.

diplomatic
[ˌdɪpləˈmætɪk]

(a.) 外交的；（避免刺激或攻击到对方）**小心翼翼的**
Teachers need to be very **diplomatic** when dealing with the parents of the kids they teach.

syllabus
[ˈsɪləbəs]

(n.) **教学（课程）大纲**
All of the information that you need to know for this course is on the **syllabus**.

methodology
[ˌmeθəˈdɒlədʒi]

(n.) 方法论；**教学法**
The grammar translation **methodology** for teaching language is very outdated.

scrutiny
[ˈskruːtɪ(ə)ni]

(n.) 监视；**监察**
The Education Department often comes under **scrutiny** for not always working in the best interests of teachers.

expertise
[ˌekspɜːˈtiːz]

(n.) 专业技能；**专业知识**
A Master's Degree by research is beneficial in gaining **expertise** in a certain field.

framework
[ˈfreɪmwɜːk]

(n.) **架构**
The subjects learnt at school provide the basic **framework** for future success.

consultation
[ˌkɒnsəlˈteɪʃən]

(n.) **咨询**；协议；协商会
Course **consultation** hours at our school are 9:00 am to 12:00 pm.

MP3-069

trend
[trend]

(n.) 趋势，流行

The recent **trend** towards e-learning has created countless new opportunities for those involved in education.

discretion
[dɪˈskreʃən]

(n.) 斟酌、处理的权限

Although there is a course outline, the final content of classes is left to the **discretion** of the teachers as ultimately they know what their students' weaknesses and needs are.

cultivate
[ˈkʌltɪ(ə)veɪt]

(v.) 耕作；栽培

The purpose of education is to not only learn things, but also **cultivate** in young learners the ability to think for themselves.

flunk
[flʌŋk]

(v.) 未通过，不及格

The reason I **flunked** that class was I was very sick that semester.

mock
[mɒk]

(v.) 嘲笑，挖苦 (a.) 模拟的，假装的

It's difficult to control those students who **mock** teachers.

trimester
[traɪˈmestəʳ]

(n.) 三学期制

Their summer break starts very late because their school is on a **trimester** schedule.

dormitory
[ˈdɔːmɪ(ə)təri]

(n.) 寝室；宿舍

In my freshman year I lived in a **dormitory** because it was the best way of meeting new people.

vocational
[vəʊˈkeɪʃənəl]

(a.) 职业的，专业技术上的
My brother went to Whitewater Community College to receive **vocational** training in how to be an electrician.

homestay
[ˈhəʊmsteɪ]

(n.)（居住在）寄宿家庭
When Lyn travelled to China she chose to live in a **homestay** with a Chinese family. Because of that, her Chinese improved a lot.

trainee
[treɪˈniː]

(n.) 受训者
IBM recently hired twenty new recruits for their executive-**trainee** programme.

☑☑☐ 精选单词 **Specialised vocabulary used in the IELTS Test**

ostracise
[ˈɒstrəsaɪz]

(v.) 排挤，排斥
Overweight children are being increasingly **ostracised** at schools throughout the country.

acquirement
[əˈkwaɪəmənt]

(n.) 取得，获得
The **acquirement** of knowledge is a life-long pursuit.

reshuffle
[riːˈʃʌfəl]

(n.) 重洗（纸牌）；改组，人事调整
With the retirement of one of the senior teachers, a **reshuffle** was needed in the coordinating team.

modern phenomenon
[ˈmɒdn fiˈnɒmɪ(ə)nən]

(n.) 现代的现象
Completing college education is a **modern phenomenon** in Asia.

MP3-070

impetus
[ˈɪmpɪ(ə)təs]

(n.) 原动力；刺激

His unwavering enthusiasm was a very large **impetus** for us to go forward with this plan.

■ 补充单词：常见学制

- kindergarten [ˈkɪndəˌgɑːtən] 幼儿园
- elementary school [ˌelɪ(ə)ˈmentəri skuːl] 小学
- secondary school [ˈsekəndri skuːl] 中等学校，中学（等同于high school）
- university [ˌjuːnɪ(ə)ˈvɜːsɪ(ə)ti] 大学
- undergraduate [ˌʌndəˈgrædʒʊɪ(ə)t] 大学生
- postgraduate [ˌpəʊstˈgrædʒʊɪ(ə)t] 研究生

MP3-071

Family · Children

☑☑☑ 高频单词 Most frequently used vocabulary in the IELTS Test

gender
[ˈdʒendəʳ]

(n.) 性别
Children of both **genders** are being encouraged to take an interest in cooking at school.

idolise
[ˈaɪdəlaɪz]

(v.) 把…当偶像崇拜
The younger generation tend to **idolise** pop stars and celebrities.

peer pressure
[pɪəʳ ˈpreʃəʳ]

(n.) 来自同辈的压力
Peer pressure was stated as the main cause for youngsters experimenting with drugs and alcohol.

household
[ˈhaʊshəʊld]

(n.) 家庭；（住在一起的）家人
If a woman's social life is limited to the **household**, she'll go crazy.

marital
[ˈmærɪtəl]

(a.) 婚姻的
Her mother is inadvertently causing them to have a lot of **marital** problems.

vulnerability
[ˌvʌlnərəˈbɪlɪti]

(n.)（身心上）容易受伤，易受影响
The **vulnerability** of children who have unmonitored access to the Internet has become more evident recently.

MP3-072

vulnerable
[ˈvʌlnərəbəl]

(a.) 脆弱的，易受伤害或影响的

Children are particularly **vulnerable** to disease because their bodies have not developed an immunity to the germs and bacteria.

同 susceptible [səˈseptəbəl] (a.) 易受影响的，感情丰富的

impressionable
[ɪmˈpreʃənəbəl]

(a.) 易受影响的（尤指年轻人）

Due to the **impressionable** nature of the minds of youngsters, film producers are being urged to reflect more as to the suitability of the content of films which are aimed at minors.

prenuptial
[ˌpriːˈnʌpʃəl]

(a.) 婚前的

Due to an increase in divorce rates, couples are being urged to sign a **prenuptial** agreement prior to marriage.

搭 prenuptial agreement 婚前协议

accountable
[əˈkaʊntəbəl]

(a.)（对自己的决定或行为）负有责任的

Recent legislation passed by the government will ensure that parents will be held **accountable** for their children.

distraction
[dɪˈstrækʃən]

(n.) 分心，精神涣散；令人分心的事物

TV is often seen as a **distraction** to young children who could alternatively be doing more productive activities.

派 distract [dɪˈstrækt] (v.) 使分心

anxiety
[æŋˈzaɪəti]

(n.) 焦虑；渴望

Soon-to-be parents are often overwhelmed by **anxieties** when preparing for the birth of their first child.

empathy
[ˈempəθi]

(n.) 同理心，移情作用

He doesn't have any **empathy** for anything; the only thing he cares about is himself.

praise
[preɪz]

(n.) 赞美，夸奖 (v.) 称赞

He never hesitates to give me **praise** for my cooking.

single-parent
[ˈsɪŋgəl ˈpeərənt]

(a.) 单亲的

Single-parent families usually require more social services because they are often mothers who cannot work and take care of their children at the same time.

bring up
[brɪŋ ʌp]

(v.) 养育

My parents **brought** me **up** to be an independent and hard-working adult.

同 raise [rez] (v.) 养育

upbringing
[ˈʌpˌbrɪŋɪŋ]

(n.) 养育，教养

Children who behave badly in school probably do so due to a poor **upbringing**.

orphan
[ˈɔːfən]

(n.) 孤儿

The recent civil war has resulted in a considerable number of children becoming **orphans**.

puberty
[ˈpjuːbəti]

(n.) 青春期

Puberty is considered to be a pivotal period in the development of a child's character.

adolescent
[ˌædəˈlesənt]

(a.) 青春期的 (n.) 青少年

During his **adolescent** years, he was a big troublemaker.

adolescence
[ˌædəˈlesəns]

(n.) 青春期

I had a lot of problems when I was going through **adolescence** because I was no longer a child and not yet an adult.

MP3-073

dependant
[dɪˈpendənt]

(n.) 需依赖他人者；被照顾者

It wasn't until after I graduated from college that I was no longer considered by the government to be a **dependant** of my parents.

authoritarian
[ɔːˌθɒrɪˈteəriən]

(a.) 权威的；独裁的

Her parents are very **authoritarian**. They never let her visit her friends or have her friends over.

lenient
[ˈliːniənt]

(a.) 不严厉的，宽厚的

I wish my parents were more **lenient**. They never let me do anything I want to do.

resemblance
[rɪˈzembləns]

(n.)（尤指外貌）相似

The **resemblance** between him and his father is striking. They have the same dark eyebrows and long nose.

shelter
[ˈʃeltəʳ]

(n.) 庇护所；遮风避雨的地方

In addition to food and **shelter**, parents should provide the love and affection that young children need.

supervision
[ˌsuːpəˈvɪʒən]

(n.) 监督

If young children don't have proper **supervision** while they are outside, they will very easily get themselves into dangerous situations.

rebelliousness
[rɪˈbeljəsnəs]

(n.) 反抗（期），叛逆（期）

In the **rebelliousness** of my youth, I never listened to my parents. I was a very defiant child.

relative
[ˈrelətɪv]

(n.) 亲戚

My **relatives** on my mum's side all used to be farmers but now have jobs in the city.

abuse
[əˈbjuːs]

(n.) 虐待；滥用

As a child he suffered verbal **abuse** from both his mother and his grandmother.

abusive
[əˈbjuːsɪv]

(a.) 虐待的，暴力相向的；谩骂的

If your husband is **abusive** to you or your children, you should seriously consider ending the marriage.

domestic violence
[dəˈmestɪk ˈvaɪələns]

(n.) 家庭暴力

Domestic violence is a serious problem in many societies no matter what societies' views are towards it.

abortion
[əˈbɔːʃən]

(n.) 堕胎

Abortion is a very controversial topic in America. It is currently legal but many people think that **abortion** should be illegal.

generation gap
[ˌdʒenəˈreɪʃən gæp]

(n.) 代沟

Because of the **generation gap** between my mum and I, she rarely understands why I make the decisions I do.

toddler
[ˈtɒdləʳ]

(n.) 初学或刚会走路的小孩

When he was a **toddler**, he used to accidentally bump into furniture.

triplet
[ˈtrɪplət]

(n.) 三胞胎

I can't imagine how difficult it would be to have twins, let alone **triplets**.

MP3-074

brat
[bræt]

(n.) 小家伙；淘气的小孩

My little sister is such a **brat**! I can't stand her!

family ties
[ˈfæməli taɪz]

(n.) 家庭关系

My **family ties** are very strong, which is why it's hard for me not to be home this Christmas.

tenant
[ˈtenənt]

(n.) 房客，承租人

The **tenants** of the property next to us are very loud. Not only I but also the landlord wants them evicted.

livelihood
[ˈlaɪvlihʊd]

(n.) 生计，生活

The only way to make a good **livelihood** in America nowadays is to have a university degree.

influential
[ˌɪnfluˈenʃəl]

(a.) 有很大影响（力）的

Children often struggle to lead their own life as a direct result of parents being very **influential** in the decision-making process of the significant stages of kids' lives.

flat
[flæt]

(n.)〈英〉公寓 (a.) 平坦的

Our **flat** in London is part of a building that is over a hundred years old.

搭 bachelor flat 单身公寓

estate
[ɪˈsteɪt]

(n.) 一大片土地，地产；财产

Part of the **estate** that my father inherited from my grandfather included a lake-side vacation home.

搭 estate agent 房地产经纪人

utilities
[juː'tɪlɪ(ə)tiz]

(n.) 水电、天然气等公共事业

The expense of our **utilities** adds up to be a tenth of our rent every month.

day care
[deɪ keəʳ]

(n.) 日间照顾（常指日间托儿所）

When I am a father, I do not want to put my children in **day care**. I am going to quit my job so I can take care of them myself.

preschool
['priːskuːl]

(n.) 托儿所，幼儿园 (a.) 学龄前的

When Tommy entered **preschool**, he was only three years old.

hang out
[hæŋ aʊt]

(v.) 停留；〈俗语〉混，玩乐

Most of the time when Tom goes over to his friends' house to **hang out**, they end up playing video games.

middle-aged
['mɪdl 'eɪdʒd]

(a.) 中年的

When I am **middle-aged**, I hope to have a stable family life and career.

retired
[rɪ'taɪəd]

(a.) 退休的

After Ted's parents **retired**, they sold their farm and bought a smaller house in town because it was more convenient.

派 retirement [rɪ'taɪəmənt] (n.) 退休，退休生活

pension
['penʃən]

(n.) 津贴，养老金；退休金

Teachers' salaries may not be very high, but after they retire, the **pension** they receive is more than enough to live on.

搭 live on a pension 以退休金、养老金维生

MP3-075

go grey
[gəʊ greɪ]

(v.) 渐渐变老（发色变灰白）

Most men don't try to hide the fact they are **going grey**. However some will dye it another colour.

look after
[lʊk ˈɑːftəʳ]

(v.) 照顾

I do not have enough time to **look after** my parents as well as my three children!

furnished apartment
[ˈfɜːnɪʃt əˈpɑːtmənt]

(n.) 附家具的出租公寓

Nick is hoping to find a **furnished apartment** near his school because he does not have enough money to buy furniture.

split up
[splɪt ʌp]

(v.) 分手

Gina and Andy mutually agreed to **split up** but that did not stop them from feeling sad after doing so.

amenities
[əˈmiːnɪ(ə)tis]

(n.) 设施，设备

Marie's house has many **amenities**, including a spacious kitchen, terrace and bathroom in the master bedroom.

garage
[ˈgærɪdʒ]

(n.) 车库

There is not enough room in our two-car **garage** for both cars and the family boat to park in.

balcony
[ˈbælkəni]

(n.) 阳台

The view from Anthony's **balcony** looks out onto a valley of deciduous trees with a river running through it.

cuddle
[ˈkʌdl]

(v.) 拥抱

Research indicates that a mother's affection is important for a young child's development. Therefore, you should **cuddle** your child often.

companion
[kəmˈpænjən]

(n.) 同伴，伴侣

Hillary doesn't want to get married but she says that it would be nice to have a **companion** once in a while.

physical abuse
[ˈfɪzɪkəl əˈbjuːs]

(n.) 身体的虐待

The home is not a place for **physical abuse**.

mistreat
[mɪsˈtriːt]

(v.) 虐待

The manner in which he **mistreats** his wife is very disturbing. Every day when he gets back from work he yells at her if she has not prepared dinner for him yet.

step relations
[step rɪˈleɪʃənz]

(n.) 继父母的关系

It's more and more common for people to have **step relations** these days because of the high divorce rates.

intimacy
[ˈɪntɪ(ə)məsi]

(n.) 亲密（关系）；亲近

It is hard for her to have **intimacy** with men because she has been hurt and abused too many times.

intervention
[ˌɪntəˈvenʃən]

(n.) 介入；干预

Without your **intervention**, I would have never been able to stop him from hitting me.

MP3-076

innocence
[ˈɪnəsəns]

(n.) 无知，天真；无辜

Her childlike **innocence** made it very hard for anyone to say anything even remotely harsh to her.

tragedy
[ˈtrædʒɪ(ə)di]

(n.) 悲剧；惨案

The father's car accident was a **tragedy** for the Lu family, after which they were unable to sustain any resemblance of a normal lifestyle.

abandoned
[əˈbændənd]

(a.) 被抛弃的

The TV station is holding an event that will heighten awareness of the plight of **abandoned** children that grow up in orphanages by sending them to Disneyland along with their favourite celebrities.

aggression
[əˈgreʃən]

(n.) 侵略；冒犯别人的言行举止

He found it difficult to control his **aggression** after having a few drinks.

remedy
[ˈremɪ(ə)di]

(n.) 治疗法；补救法

The only **remedy** for a cold is lots of hot liquids and plenty of rest.

adulthood
[ˈædʌlthʊd]

(n.) 成年

I don't really know at what age **adulthood** starts, but I do know that I have been feeling like more of an 'adult' since I graduated from college.

childhood
[ˈtʃaɪldhʊd]

(n.) 童年

She has many happy memories of her **childhood**.

solitary
[ˈsɒlɪ(ə)təri]

(a.) 单独的，独来独往的

It was hard for her to get used to being married because before that she had led a **solitary** lifestyle.

派 solitude [ˈsɒlɪtjuːd] (n.) 独处，单独一人

maternity
[məˈtɜːnɪ(ə)ti]

(a.) 怀孕的，孕妇的 (n.) 母性

The **maternity** store on the corner of Benjamin Street sells **maternity** books as well as clothes.

参 give birth 生产

conceive
[kənˈsiːv]

(v.) 怀孕，怀胎；构想（计划或主意）

Some couples try to **conceive** children for many years before they are successful.

搭 conceive a child = be expecting a child = be pregnant 怀孕，怀胎

infant
[ˈɪnfənt]

(n.) 婴儿

The **infant** mortality rate has decreased in many regions due to the increased affordability of prescription drugs.

搭 infant mortality rate 婴儿夭折率

traumatise
[ˈtrɔːmətaɪz]

(v.) 使受到创伤

I didn't mean to **traumatise** you with what I said! You shouldn't take what I say so seriously.

☑☑☐ 精选单词 Specialised vocabulary used in the IELTS Test

widower
[ˈwɪdəʊəʳ]

(n.) 鳏夫

He became a **widower** two years ago when his wife tragically died in a car crash.

派 widow [ˈwɪdəʊ] (n.) 寡妇，遗孀

MP3-077

nuclear family
[ˈnjuːkliəʳ ˈfæməli]

(n.) 核心家庭，小家庭

In Western countries, while **nuclear families** are seen as the norm, more and more children are growing up in dysfunctional families.

extended family
[ɪkˈstendɪ(ə)d ˈfæməli]

(n.) 大家庭

I live in an **extended family** in a traditional Chinese house.

juvenile
[ˈdʒuːvənaɪl]

(a.) 青少年的 (n.) 青少年（在英国，18岁以下称为 juvenile）

The prosecution is endeavouring to have the 17-year-old, who committed that murder, tried in adult court rather than **juvenile** court because of the severity of the crime and the apparent maturity of the defendant.

juvenile delinquency
[ˈdʒuːvənaɪl dɪˈlɪŋkwənsi]

(n.) 青少年犯罪

The rates of **juvenile delinquency** in London has been increasing over the past twenty years.

sibling
[ˈsɪblɪŋ]

(n.) 兄弟姊妹

I have five **siblings**: two older brothers, one younger brother, an older sister and a younger sister.

foster family
[ˈfɒstəʳ ˈfæməli]

(n.) 寄养家庭

My **foster family** never treated me like I was any different from their own children.

second-class citizen
[ˈsekənd klɑːs ˈsɪtɪ(ə)zən]

(n.) 次等公民

Many minorities in the United States are treated like **second-class citizens**.

spouse
[spaʊs]

(n.) 配偶

If it weren't for the support that my **spouse** gives me, I would not be able to face the day's challenges.

baby boom
[ˈbeɪbi buːm]

(n.) 婴儿潮

After World War II there was a **baby boom** caused by all the soldiers returning home, getting married and having babies.

population density
[ˌpɒpjʊˈleɪʃən ˈdensɪ(ə)ti]

(n.) 人口密度

The **population density** is much greater in Manhattan than in other parts of New York City.

distribution of population
[ˌdɪstrɪ(ə)ˈbjuʃən əv ˌpɒpjʊˈleɪʃən]

(n.) 人口分布

The **distribution of population** in Australia is very uneven. Most of the population lives along the East Coast.

offspring
[ˈɒfˌsprɪŋ]

(n.) 子女，子孙；刚出生的小动物

That cat's **offspring** are all having health problems.

dwelling
[ˈdwelɪŋ]

(n.) 住处；寓所

The place where you make your **dwelling** is the place that you will be most attached to.

paediatrics
[ˌpiːdiˈætrɪks]

(n.) 小儿科

Our doctor decided to study **paediatrics** medicine because she enjoys being around children.

folks
[fəʊks]

(n.) 父母亲；特定的一群人

I'm kind of scared to take my girlfriend home to see my **folks**.

MP3-078

twenty-somethings
['twenti 'sʌmθɪŋz]

(n.) 二十几岁

People who are in their **twenty-somethings** tend to be very concerned about who they will get married to.

thirty-somethings
['θɜːti 'sʌmθɪŋz]

(n.) 三十几岁

When I was in my **thirty-somethings**, I was consumed by my career.

porch
[pɔːtʃ]

(n.) 前廊

Children like to sit on the **porch** and watch the world go by.

guardian
['gɑːdiən]

(n.) 监护人

You must consider carefully whether you are able to be the **guardian** of our child because it is a big responsibility. It means that if we, his parents, pass away, you will be responsible for raising him.

will
[wɪl]

(n.) 遗嘱；意志力

Grandpa's **will** stated that his estate should be split evenly between his four children.

bungalow
['bʌŋgələʊ]

(n.) 平房，别墅

There are no tall buildings in that neighbourhood. Instead it is filled with small **bungalows** that were built fifty years ago.

heterosexual
[ˌhetərə'seksjʊəl]

(n.) 异性恋（者）

Homosexuals argue that only allowing **heterosexuals** to get married is another form of prejudice.

参 homosexual [ˌhəʊməʊ'seksjuəl] (n.) 同性恋（者）

kinship
[ˈkɪnʃɪp]

(n.) 亲属关系，相似、亲近的感觉

If it were not for the bond of **kinship**, I would never return to my hometown.

nurture
[ˈnɜːtʃəʳ]

(v.) (n.) 教养，养育

The home is the place where children should be **nurtured** from a young age all the way up until they are old enough to be financially independent.

autism
[ˈɔːtɪzəm]

(n.) 自闭（症）

Professor Lin's son is autistic. His son's **autism** is sometimes a big source of hardship for the family.

派 autistic [ɔːˈtɪstɪk] (a.) 自闭的，孤僻的

interpersonal
[ˌɪntəˈpɜːsənəl]

(a.) 人际关系的，人与人之间的

He is lacking in **interpersonal** skills and so has a hard time making new friends.

temperament
[ˈtempərəmənt]

(n.) 性情

My dad has a very mild **temperament**. He is rarely bothered by anything that we do.

派 temper [ˈtempəʳ] (n.) 脾气

- ►lose/keep one's temper (with sb) 发脾气/忍住怒气
- ►have a quick temper 容易发怒，急性子

separation anxiety
[ˌsepəˈreɪʃən æŋˈzaɪəti]

(n.) 分离焦虑（症）（尤指儿童与父母的分离）

If I move half a world away, my mum will definitely suffer from **separation anxiety**.

prodigy
[ˈprɒdɪdʒi]

(n.) 奇才，天才（尤指未成年的孩子）

When my son was young he was a math **prodigy**, which paved the way for him to be a professor of electrical engineering at Princeton University.

MP3-079

myopia
[maɪ'əʊpiə]

(n.) 近视；短视近利

She had to buy a new pair of glasses to correct her **myopia**.

judicious
[dʒuː'dɪʃəs]

(a.) 明智的；深谋远虑的

Parents need a very **judicious** approach when handling disputes between siblings.

cohabit
[kəʊ'hæbɪt]

(v.) 同居

In many countries after couples have **cohabited** for a certain number of years they are considered married.

☑☐☐ 挑战单词 Sophisticated vocabulary used in the IELTS Test

filial
['fɪliəl]

(a.) 子女的

Filial piety is the idea that parents deserve the respect of their children and that children should do everything that their parents say.

搭 filial piety 孝心，孝道

tug-of-love
[tʌg əv lʌv]

(a.) 争夺孩子监护权的

They have been involved in a **tug-of-love** battle for two years.

formative years
['fɔːmətɪv jɪəz]

(n.) 性格养成期

It is important to teach children proper manners and good morals during their **formative years**.

depopulation
[diːˌpɒpjʊ'leɪʃən]

(n.) 人口减少

Depopulation is a major threat to the prosperity of many European nations.

派 depopulate [ˌdiː'pɒpjʊleɪt] (v.) 人口减少

Law • Crime

☑☑☑ 高频单词 Most frequently used vocabulary in the IELTS Test

fraud
[frɔːd]

(n.) 诈欺；**仿冒品；** 骗子

Due to the ease of reproduction of passports and bankcards, **fraud** is becoming increasingly widespread.

参 pirated [ˈpaɪrətɪd] (a.) 盗版的
▶pirated CD 盗版光盘

embezzlement
[ɪmˈbezəlmənt]

(n.) **盗用公款**

The CEO was arrested for **embezzlement** of the company's funds.

派 embezzle [ɪmˈbezəl] (v.) 挪用、侵占款项

smuggling
[ˈsmʌglɪŋ]

(n.) **走私**（罪）

Cross-border **smuggling** is one of the biggest challenges facing law enforcement officials.

参 law enforcement officials 执法人员

theft
[θeft]

(n.) **偷窃，窃盗**

The number of **thefts**, from both businesses and private residences, has decreased over the past five years.

counterfeit
[ˈkaʊntəfɪt]

(v.) **伪造** (n.) 伪造品 (a.) 仿冒的

Because of new technology, bank notes are becoming harder and harder to **counterfeit**.

conviction
[kənˈvɪkʃən]

(n.) **定罪；** 强烈的信念或意见

The prisoner is trying to overturn his **conviction** on the basis that the witness' testimony was flawed.

MP3-081

convict
[kən'vɪkt]

(v.) 宣判某人有罪

He was **convicted** of manslaughter, much to the relief of the victim's family.

defendant
[dɪ'fendənt]

(n.) 被告

The **defendant** in this trial has consistently claimed that she was not present at the crime scene on the night of the murder.

jury
['dʒʊəri]

(n.) 陪审团；评判委员会

It will be up to the **jury** to decide whether she is innocent or guilty.

testify
['testɪ(ə)faɪ]

(v.)（出庭）作证

The witness **testified** that she saw the defendant at the crime scene.

sentence
['sentəns]

(n.) (v.) 判决，判刑

Bearing in mind that this was a major offence, the **sentence** of 3 years in prison is quite lenient.

搭 death sentence = death penalty = capital punishment 死刑
life sentence 无期徒刑
suspended sentence 缓刑

immunity
[ɪ'mjuːnəti]

(n.) 豁免权；免疫力

The captured terrorist agreed to cooperate in exchange for **immunity** from prosecution.

搭 diplomatic immunity 外交豁免权
immunity from sth 豁免于…
immunity to/against sth 对…具免疫力

entrapment
[ɪn'træpmənt]

(n.)（非法）**诱捕**

The lawyer accused the police of using **entrapment** to gain evidence against his client.

victim
['vɪktɪ(ə)m]

(n.) **受害者，被害人**

The **victim** in this murder case received multiple gunshot wounds to the head.

offender
[ə'fendə^r]

(n.) **违法者；**无礼的人

The number of traffic **offenders** has increased over the past three years.

solicitor
[sə'lɪsɪ(ə)tə^r]

(n.) **事务（准备）律师**（用于英国与澳洲，律师对于案件仅做准备工作与给予建议，可以代表出席较轻微的案子）

My **solicitor** checked the contract before I signed it.

abortion
[ə'bɔːʃən]

(n.) **堕胎，人工流产**

She is considering having an **abortion** because she does not think that she is ready to have a child.

accuse
[ə'kjuːz]

(v.) **指控；**谴责

The police **accused** the youth of using a false name and resisting arrest.

barrister
['bærɪ(ə)stə^r]

(n.) **讼务律师**（在英国、澳洲以及一些其他的国家，除了法庭案件外，他们可以进行高等法院审理的诉讼案件）

Henry Sykes QC's services as a **barrister** have been in demand ever since he won the 'Babies in Wheelie Bins' case.

MP3-082

parole
[pə'rəʊl]

(n.) 假释

Before you can be released on **parole**, you have to prove that you sincerely regret having committed your crime.

verdict
['vɜːdɪkt]

(n.) 裁决；结论

The **verdict** of this case will be delivered from the jury at one o'clock this afternoon.

lenient
['liːniənt]

(a.) （过于）宽大的；仁慈的

I feel that the sentence given to that criminal was too **lenient**.

wrongdoer
['rɒŋ'duːəʳ]

(n.) 做坏事的人，犯罪的人

In this case it is still not clear who the **wrongdoer** is.

burglary
['bɜːgləri]

(n.) 入屋窃盗（罪）

Whoever committed that **burglary** was not very smart as they didn't take any of the famous paintings.

robbery
['rɒbəri]

(n.) 抢劫

A local man was arrested on Tuesday for the **robbery** of Big Jim's Bakery.

shoplifter
['ʃɒpˌlɪftəʳ]

(n.) 商店扒手

My guess is that most people have been a **shoplifter** at least once in their life, whether it was intentional or it happened inadvertently.

rapist
['reɪpɪ(ə)st]

(n.) 强奸犯

The serial **rapist** Patches O'Toole initially denied molesting Ms Dugan outside her Tucas Street home but later confessed.

hooligan
[ˈhuːlɪ(ə)gən]

(n.) 流氓，恶棍

Violence committed by soccer **hooligans** on rival fans once again marred Saturday night's game.

hijack
[ˈhaɪdʒæk]

(v.) 绑架；劫持（飞机等）(n.) 劫持事件

Because of the much higher airport security that exists these days, it's considerably more difficult to **hijack** a plane.

forger
[ˈfɔːdʒəʳ]

(n.)（钱或文件的）伪造者

You should shred old cheques. You don't want to let a **forger** see your signature.

terrorism
[ˈterərɪzəm]

(n.) 恐怖主义，恐怖攻击

Many people believe that **terrorism** has become worse after the Iraq War started.

terrorist
[ˈterərɪst]

(n.) 恐怖分子

One of the government's top goals is to capture **terrorists**.

assassination
[əˌsæsɪ(ə)ˈneɪʃən]

(n.) 暗杀，刺杀

President Reagan was the target of an **assassination** attempt. Thankfully the assassin was unsuccessful.

corruption
[kəˈrʌpʃən]

(n.) 贪污，腐败

Frequent changes in the party that has political control aid in the prevention of **corruption**.

custody
[ˈkʌstədi]

(n.) 监护；拘留

He is being held in **custody** until the trial starts.

MP3-083

detention
[dɪ'tenʃən]

(n.) 拘留

The **detention** centres in Australia have often come under fire from human rights activists for the appalling treatment of asylum seekers.

commit
[kə'mɪt]

(v.) 犯（罪）

I can't believe that he **committed** that crime as he was always so friendly to me.

legitimate
[lɪ'dʒɪtɪ(ə)mɪ(ə)t]

(a.) 合法的，正统的

The blood test will determine whether or not he is the **legitimate** father of his girlfriend's son.

obligatory
[ə'blɪgətəri]

(a.) 义务的

Taxes are an **obligatory** fee that must be paid every year.

compulsory
[kəm'pʌlsəri]

(a.) 强制的

I don't believe that school attendance before the age of six should be **compulsory**.

taboo
[tə'buː]

(a.) 忌讳的 (n.) 禁忌

Despite the prevalence of rape and abortion in society, it is still seen as a **taboo** subject.

lawsuit
['lɔːsuːt]

(n.) 诉讼

We intend to file a **lawsuit** against a rival company for stealing a software application our company has been working on.

plea
[pliː]

(n.) 请求；答辩；借口

The accused man entered a **plea** of not guilty for the crime of kidnapping.

prosecute
[ˈprɒsɪkjuːt]

(v.) 起诉；告发，检举

The attorney general is going to **prosecute** the suspect in last week's burglary.

plaintiff
[ˈpleɪntɪ(ə)f]

(n.) 原告

The **plaintiff** accused the defendant of borrowing two thousand dollars from her but never paying her back.

acquit
[əˈkwɪt]

(v.) 宣判无罪，无罪开释

The criminal was **acquitted** of all charges laid against him.

heir
[eəʳ]

(n.) 继承人

The **heir** claims that he did not receive the full amount of the inheritance.

detective
[dɪˈtektɪv]

(n.) 侦探

I hired the private **detective** because I suspected my husband of cheating on me.

patrol
[pəˈtrəʊl]

(v.) 巡逻

I would feel safer if I knew that there were policemen **patrolling** our block.

swindle
[ˈswɪndl]

(v.) (n.) 诈骗，骗取

That man is not really homeless. He is just trying to **swindle** you out of your money.

homicide
[ˈhɒmɪ(ə)saɪd]

(n.) 谋杀

The **homicide** rate in Los Angeles has dropped over the past twenty years, but the number of non-violent crimes has risen.

MP3-084

suicide
[ˈsuːɪ(ə)saɪd]

(n.) 自杀

His younger brother committed **suicide** two years ago.

▶ 字根 -cide有“杀死，毁灭”之意，例如 infanticide（杀婴罪，杀婴犯）、pesticide（杀虫剂）

detainee
[ˌdiːteɪˈniː]

(n.) 被拘禁者（尤指政治事件）

He spent ten years as a **detainee** in China.

injurious
[ɪnˈdʒʊəriəs]

(a.) 有害的，伤害的

Drunk driving is potentially **injurious** to the driver, his/her passengers and also other road users.

violation
[ˌvaɪəˈleɪʃən]

(n.) 侵犯，妨碍；违规

That parking **violation** cost him $40.

morality
[məˈrælɪ(ə)ti]

(n.) 道德

The **morality** of this country is getting worse and worse. Nowadays young people don't know what good morals are.

distort
[dɪˈstɔːt]

(v.) 扭曲，曲解

Witnesses' versions of the events of a crime can become quite **distorted** if a lot of emotional trauma was experienced.

submission
[səbˈmɪʃən]

(n.) 屈服；向法官提出的意见、看法

Lawyers made their final **submissions** for the case that has brought much media attention.

plausible
[ˈplɔːzɪ(ə)bəl]

(a.) 似乎是真的；**似合理的**

The defendant's explanation of the incident seems quite **plausible**.

negligence
[ˈneglɪdʒəns]

(n.) 疏忽；（由于不注意而发生的）**过失**

The pilot involved in last year's crash at Jandakot Airport was drunk at the time and so was jailed for **negligence**.

mischief
[ˈmɪstʃɪ(ə)f]

(n.) **伤害，危害他人的行为**

The defendant was charged with criminal **mischief** in the third degree.

indulgence
[ɪnˈdʌldʒəns]

(n.) **沉迷，放任**

There needs to be a crackdown on motorists who continue to drive after a night of alcohol **indulgence**.

incriminate
[ɪnˈkrɪmɪ(ə)neɪt]

(v.) **归罪，陷人于…罪**

Suspects may refuse to answer questions asked by police if they fear they may **incriminate** themselves.

deprive
[dɪˈpraɪv]

(v.) **剥夺**

Many prisons in developing countries **deprive** inmates of even the most basic human rights.

派 deprivation [ˌdeprɪˈveɪʃən] (n.) 剥夺

euthanasia
[ˌjuːθəˈneɪziə]

(n.) **安乐死**

Terminally ill patients in the Netherlands who want to end their lives may opt for **euthanasia** or mercy killing, as it is sometimes known.

MP3-085

exemption
[ɪg'zempʃən]

(n.) 豁免

People with severe back problems have in the past been granted **exemptions** to the law requiring all car drivers to wear seat belts.

illicit
[ɪ'lɪsɪ(ə)t]

(a.) 违法的；不被允许、接受的

The **illicit** acts that he performed while he was president didn't become public until after he had died.

invade
[ɪn'veɪd]

(v.) 侵犯，侵略

Many people were against the US Allied decision to **invade** Iraq in search of weapons of mass destruction.

magistrate
['mædʒɪ(ə)streɪt]

(n.) 长官；地方法院处理小型案件的法官

The **magistrate** sentenced the youth to 60 days of community service.

manslaughter
['mænˌslɔːtə^{r}]

(n.) 过失杀人

While it is not as serious as murder, the crime of **manslaughter** still carries a lengthy jail term for anyone convicted of it.

notorious
[nəʊ'tɔːriəs]

(a.) 恶名昭彰的

To the relief of the public, it was announced late last night that the **notorious** rapist had finally been captured and placed under arrest.

provoke
[prə'vəʊk]

(v.) 激怒，挑衅

Although it was clear that he was **provoked**, he will still be charged with manslaughter in the second degree.

rebut
[rɪ'bʌt]

(v.) 反驳

The allegations were quickly **rebutted** when the defendant took to the stand.

sanction
['sæŋkʃən]

(n.) 批准，认可；**制裁** (v.) 批准，认可；实施制裁

Because of suspicions about Iraq's nuclear and biological weapons activities, the United Nations imposed **sanctions** on the country.

violate
['vaɪəleɪt]

(v.) **违反，侵犯**

He has **violated** our school's policy on tardiness five times already. Soon we will have to consider suspending him.

☑☑☐ 精选单词 Specialised vocabulary used in the IELTS Test

misdeed
[mɪs'diːd]

(n.) 违法；**不良的行为**

I would not take this **misdeed** any further if you apologised to her and covered all of her medical expenses.

retribution
[ˌretrɪ(ə)'bjuːʃən]

(n.) **应得的惩罚，报应**

It has been known for the families of rape victims to seek **retribution** by other means if they feel the courts have failed them.

pilfer
['pɪlfəʳ]

(v.) **偷窃**

Little kids are often tempted to **pilfer** candy from the supermarket.

decree
[dɪ'kriː]

(v.) **宣判**；下达命令 (n.) 法令；命令

The judge **decreed** that the murderer had to serve a sentence of forty years before being eligible for parole.

MP3-086

tribunal
[traɪˈbjuːnl]

(n.) 特别法庭

When the **tribunal** meets tomorrow they will decide the political prisoner's fate.

litigate
[ˈlɪtɪ(ə)geɪt]

(v.) 打官司

Mr Jackson decided not to **litigate** over the story printed in last Friday's newspaper when he discovered that he knew the writer from his school days.

bobby
[ˈbɒbi]

(n.) 警察（英国旧式非正式用语）

London **bobbies** don't carry guns.

crook
[krʊk]

(n.) 骗子；坏蛋；弯曲处

Many **crooks** are caught by the cops when they start bragging about their crimes.

supposition
[ˌsʌpəˈzɪʃən]

(n.) 臆测，想象

When deciding if someone is guilty of a crime or not, one must look at the facts and not simply **supposition**.

circumspect
[ˈsɜːkəmspekt]

(a.) 小心谨慎的

One of the purposes of malpractice lawsuits is to ensure that doctors are more **circumspect**.

criminology
[ˌkrɪmɪ(ə)ˈnɒlədʒi]

(n.) 犯罪学

Recent **criminology** research shows that violent acts committed by juveniles have been on the rise.

cybercrime
[ˈsaɪbəkraɪm]

(n.) 网络犯罪

She was the victim of **cybercrime**. A hacker was able to get all of her personal information from the Internet and maxed out all of her credit cards.

flagrant
[ˈfleɪgrənt]

(a.) 明目张胆的，公然的

The **flagrant** misuse of public money by the president and his executive staff caused a scandal that shook the entire country to its foundations.

underpin
[ˌʌndəˈpɪn]

(v.) 用东西支撑；给予支持

The constitution usually **underpins** all other laws in a country.

☑□□ 挑战单词 Sophisticated vocabulary used in the IELTS Test

nefarious
[nɪˈfeəriəs]

(a.) 邪恶的，不法的

The mobsters are involved in all kinds of **nefarious** activities, such as prostitution, gambling and drugs.

People • Character • Emotion

☑☑☑ 高频单词 Most frequently used vocabulary in the IELTS Test

characteristic
[ˌkærɪ(ə)ktəˈrɪstɪk]

(n.) 特征；个人特质
She has several endearing **characteristics**: the way she flutters her eyelids and her shy laugh.
派 characterise [ˈkærɪktəraɪz] (v.) 具备…特征
►be characterised by sth 具有…特质、特征

loathe
[ləʊð]

(v.) 厌恶，憎恨
In general, most mothers **loathe** the first time that they send their children to school.

caring
[ˈkeərɪŋ]

(a.) 体贴的，乐于助人的
Possessing a **caring** and loving attitude towards one's children has been shown to be the most important factor in child rearing.

jealous
[ˈdʒeləs]

(a.) 妒忌的，吃醋的
Husbands have been known to become **jealous** of excessive affection shown by their wives to their children.

compassion
[kəmˈpæʃən]

(n.) 怜悯，同情
Compassion is the most constructive emotion which a parent can have for and foster in their children.

sustain
[səˈsteɪn]

(v.) 维持；忍受；支持
I cannot imagine how difficult it must be to **sustain** a long-distance relationship.

sustainable
[sə'steɪnəbəl]

(a.) 可维持的；可支撑的，可持续的

Their relationship was no longer **sustainable** due to his self-centred behaviour.

undergo
[ˌʌndə'gəʊ]

(v.) 经历；忍受

His lifestyle has **undergone** massive changes as a result of his new outlook on life.

stand up to
[stænd ʌp tʊ]

(v.) 勇于面对

I really admire the way he **stood up to** his classmates' claims that his beliefs were nonsense.

stick with it
[stɪk wɪθ ɪt]

(v.) 继续，坚持

If we don't **stick with it**, our competitors are going to beat us.

furious
['fjʊəriəs]

(a.) 震怒的

The way you treated me yesterday made me absolutely **furious**.

impatient
[ɪm'peɪʃənt]

(a.) 不耐烦的，没耐性的

Learning to write Chinese characters requires a lot of patience; it is definitely not for **impatient** people!

irritating
['ɪrɪ(ə)teɪtɪŋ]

(a.) 恼人的

I don't know why I find his personality so **irritating**, but it's just that every time I'm around him, he bugs me.

resent
[rɪ'zent]

(v.) 对…感到愤恨、不满

Sue **resents** the way you treated her yesterday. You should apologise to her.

MP3-088

bad-tempered
[bæd ˈtempəʳd]

(a.) 坏脾气的

I'm afraid to tell him anything because he is very **bad-tempered**.

touchy
[ˈtʌtʃi]

(a.) 易受刺激的；敏感的

She is very **touchy** so don't say anything too harsh.

craving
[ˈkreɪvɪŋ]

(n.) 渴望

Her insecurity and low self-esteem meant that she often gave into her **cravings** for fattening foods and alcohol.

派 crave [kreɪv] (v.) 渴望

possessive
[pəˈzesɪv]

(a.) 占有欲强的

Dawn's boyfriend is very **possessive**. Every time she talks to another guy, he gets jealous.

temptation
[tempˈteɪʃən]

(n.) 诱惑

I cannot resist the **temptation** to make jokes when she is on the phone with her boyfriend.

thirst
[θɜːst]

(n.) 口渴；渴望

She always has a **thirst** for travelling.

cling to
[klɪŋ tʊ]

(v.) 紧抓不放；缠着；坚持

You are too attached to your boyfriend. The more you **cling to** him, the more you will drive him away.

cross your fingers
[krɒs jəʳ ˈfɪŋgəʳz]

(v.) 希望能如愿，祈求好运

The lottery numbers are about to be announced! **Cross your fingers**!

beloved
[bɪˈlʌvɪ(ə)d]

(a.) 深爱的；挚爱的

His obsession with his **beloved** car was often the underlying cause of the arguments with his girlfriend.

short-sighted
[ʃɔːtˈsaɪtɪ(ə)d]

(a.) 短视的；近视的

Our direct boss rejected all the proposals we wrote. He is **short-sighted** to the market trends.

small-minded
[smɔːlˈmaɪndɪ(ə)d]

(a.) 心胸或思虑狭窄的

Small-minded people are the ones who put the Prime Minister in office last time. I'm not going to let it happen again.

worship
[ˈwɜːʃɪp]

(v.) 崇拜，仰慕

You love money so much. It's almost like you **worship** it.

favourite
[ˈfeɪvərɪ(ə)t]

(a.) 最喜爱的 (n.) 最喜爱的东西（人）

My **favourite** season is spring because that is when everything becomes new again.

preference
[ˈprefərəns]

(n.) 较喜爱的东西；偏好

Regarding these two plans, I don't really have a **preference**, so you can do either one and it will be fine with me.

gorgeous
[ˈgɔːdʒəs]

(a.) 华美的，高贵的；极可爱的

Your baby looks absolutely **gorgeous** in this photo.

graceful
[ˈgreɪsfəl]

(a.) 优雅的，得体的

Her manners at the table are very **graceful**.

MP3-089

irresistible
[ˌɪrɪˈzɪstɪ(ə)bəl]

(a.) 非常诱人的，让人无法抗拒的

His smile is absolutely **irresistible**. I always find myself smiling after I see him.

stunning
[ˈstʌnɪŋ]

(a.) 极漂亮的；惊为天人的

You don't have to be **stunning** to be a movie star.

tempting
[ˈtemptɪŋ]

(a.) 诱人的

Your offer is very **tempting**, but I am sorry I cannot accept it.

bittersweet
[ˌbɪtəˈswiːt]

(a.) 苦乐参半的

Her departure from Los Angeles was very **bittersweet**. She was looking forward to going to England but she knew that she would miss her friends too.

cheerful
[ˈtʃɪəfəl]

(a.) 快乐的，开朗的

Every time I see Latoya she is always so **cheerful**. I wonder what makes her so happy.

comfy
[ˈkʌmfi]

(a.) 舒适的

A **comfy** night on the sofa watching movies and eating ice cream is often in order when you are feeling upset and wanting some time alone.

content
[kənˈtent]

(a.) 满足的

If you are **content** with your present circumstances, you may lose the drive to work hard.

cosy
[ˈkəʊzi]

(a.) 亲切的，友善的

Exactly how **cosy** he was with some of his clients was often the topic of conversation among his colleagues.

delightful
[dɪˈlaɪtfəl]

(a.) 令人愉快的，欢乐的
The news of your engagement is so **delightful**!

fulfilling
[fʊlˈfɪlɪŋ]

(a.) 令人满足的，有成就感的
Being a nurse may be very hard work but it is also **fulfilling** because you get to help other people.
派 fulfillment [fʊlˈfɪlmənt] (n.) 成就（感）
参 accomplishment [əˈkʌmplɪʃmənt] (n.) 成就，完成
achievement [əˈtʃiːvmənt] (n.) 成就，功绩

giggle
[ˈgɪgəl]

(v.) 咯咯地笑；傻笑
His voice sounds so funny. I cannot help but **giggle** every time he starts talking.

grateful
[ˈgreɪtfəl]

(a.) 感激的
I am very **grateful** for your help in doing my errands while I was in hospital.

gratitude
[ˈgrætɪ(ə)tjuːd]

(n.) 感激之情；谢意
I am so grateful for your help that words cannot express my **gratitude**.

indulge
[ɪnˈdʌldʒ]

(v.) 放任；纵容
Every now and then I like to **indulge** myself with a spa and massage.

despair
[dɪˈspeəʳ]

(n.) 绝望
Please do not feel **despair** about this situation. It will get better soon.

MP3-090

optimistic
[ˌɒptɪ(ə)ˈmɪstɪk]

(a.) 乐观的

I am very **optimistic** that this situation will reach a good resolution.

ego
[ˈiːgəʊ]

(n.) 自我；自负

His big **ego** prevents him from noticing when other people need attention.

grief
[griːf]

(n.) 忧伤；悲恸

The **grief** that Lyn felt after her husband died was so despairing that I couldn't stand to see her like that.

hurtful
[ˈhɜːtfəl]

(a.) 伤人的

The way that you treated me this morning was very **hurtful** to my feelings.

lonesome
[ˈləʊnsəm]

(a.) 孤单的

One of the problems about living in another country is that it is very easy to feel **lonesome**.

mourning
[ˈmɔːnɪŋ]

(n.) 服丧；悲恸

After Lyn's husband died, she went through a period of **mourning** that lasted for almost a year.

offence
[əˈfens]

(n.) 犯罪行为；污辱、攻击等令人不悦的举动

Don't worry; what you said didn't offend me. And if you ever do say anything that causes an **offence**, I will tell you.

outrage
[ˈaʊtreɪdʒ]

(n.) 愤怒，震惊

She expressed her **outrage** over how unaffectionate her husband had become.

pessimism
[ˈpesɪ(ə)mɪzəm]

(n.) 悲观

He is always so negative. So much so that his **pessimism** makes other people around him also feel hopeless.

regretful
[rɪˈgretfəl]

(a.) 懊悔的，悔不当初的

She sounded rather **regretful** over the whole incident and promised that nothing of that order would ever happen again.

awesome
[ˈɔːsəm]

(a.) 感到可怕的；令人敬畏、佩服的；〈美〉好极了

The way he handled the situation was rather admirable; in fact, it was nothing short of **awesome**.

dread
[dred]

(n.) (v.) 恐惧，担心

The news about my mother's sickness filled me with **dread**.

Sue **dreaded** finding out the results of her blood test.

dreadful
[ˈdredfəl]

(a.) 糟糕的；令人震惊的

There is nothing more **dreadful** than losing your job.

fearful
[ˈfɪəfəl]

(a.) 担忧的；惊吓的

You cannot live your life being **fearful** of what may come. You must be courageous instead.

frightened
[ˈfraɪtnd]

(a.) 受惊吓的

James was very **frightened** by the scary movie.

panic
[ˈpænɪk]

(v.) 惊慌；激动；失控

Young children tend to **panic** at the thought of going to the doctor to get their shots done.

MP3-091

daring
[ˈdeərɪŋ]

(a.) 勇敢的；大胆的

My girlfriend is always encouraging me to try new things, but I am not as **daring** as she is.

humble
[ˈhʌmbəl]

(a.) 谦逊的；卑微的

She is so **humble** about her great performance.

flatter
[ˈflætəʳ]

(v.) 奉承，讨好

If you **flatter** Ted too much, his ego will get bigger.

anxious
[ˈæŋkʃəs]

(a.) 焦虑不安的；渴望的

Every time the boss walks into the room, his secretary becomes more **anxious**.

oppressive
[əˈpresɪv]

(a.) 难以忍受的；压迫的，不公平的

The government's religious restrictions are **oppressive** for many Christians.

tension
[ˈtenʃən]

(n.) 紧张

I hope the fact that I am dating your ex-girlfriend doesn't cause any **tension** between us.

extrovert
[ˈekstrəvɜːt]

(n.) 个性外向的人

I think that most of the time I am an **extrovert**, but sometimes I can feel pretty introverted.

introvert
[ˈɪntrəvɜːt]

(n.) 个性内向的人

Their son was such an **introvert** that he found it extremely difficult to make any new friends.

admirable
[ˈædmərəbəl]

(a.) 令人钦佩的；极好的

The way he handled that difficult situation was very **admirable**.

adorable
[əˈdɔːrəbəl]

(a.) 值得爱慕的；（常指婴孩或小动物）极可爱的

Her baby daughter is so **adorable**!

affectionate
[əˈfekʃənɪ(ə)t]

(a.) 亲切的；有感情的

I feel that you are not **affectionate** enough. If you showed me more affection, our marriage would be much happier.

absent-minded
[ˈæbsənt ˈmaɪndɪ(ə)d]

(a.) 心不在焉的

I would not be very good at watching young children because I am too **absent-minded**.

disgrace
[dɪsˈgreɪs]

(n.) 丢脸，耻辱

If you marry this kind of man, you will bring **disgrace** upon the entire family.

soothing
[ˈsuːðɪŋ]

(a.) 抚慰的；使人放松、宽心的

My favourite way to relax after a long day at work is to take a nice, long, **soothing** bath.

ethical
[ˈeθɪkəl]

(a.) 道德的

Ethical conduct is important in many professions including journalism, medicine and law.

glamorous
[ˈglæmərəs]

(a.) 富有魅力的；迷人的

I can never hope to be as **glamorous** as that movie star.

MP3-092

☑☑☐ 精选单词 **Specialised vocabulary used in the IELTS Test**

impassive
[ɪmˈpæsɪv]

(a.) 无动于衷的，毫无感觉的

How can you remain **impassive** after hearing the news of her sickness?

surly
[ˈsɜːli]

(a.) 脾气坏的，不友善的

The **surly** cowboy strolled up to the bar, slammed his mug down on the counter, and yelled: 'Give me one more!'

yearning
[ˈjɜːnɪŋ]

(n.) 渴望；怀念

Because I am so far away from my hometown, I always feel this constant **yearning** to return home.

alluring
[əˈluːrɪŋ]

(a.) 诱人的

The items in the store display are meant to be very **alluring** to the pedestrians passing by.

endearing
[ɪnˈdɪərɪŋ]

(a.) 惹人喜爱的；可爱的

The way that he talks about his girlfriend is very **endearing**. It's as if she's everything in the world to him.

glorious
[ˈglɔːriəs]

(a.) 光荣的

The feeling of euphoria that he felt after the victory was absolutely **glorious**.

blissful
[ˈblɪsfəl]

(a.) 幸福的，喜悦的

As soon as I sat in the hot tub, I felt a **blissful** feeling of relaxation.

downcast
[ˈdaʊnkɑːst]

(a.) 垂头丧气的；忧伤的

Every time I see him he looks **downcast**. At first I thought that it was because he is always sad, but actually that's just the way his face is.

self-important
[ˌself ɪmˈpɔːtənt]

(a.) 自我中心的

His **self-important** manner prevents him from making good friends.

smug
[smʌg]

(a.) 自满的，沾沾自喜的，自鸣得意的

Ever since he graduated from Harvard Law School, he has been much more **smug**.

resolute
[ˈrezəluːt]

(a.)（行为或决定）坚决的，坚定的

My stance on this position is **resolute**. There is no way that you will be able to change my mind.

scrupulous
[ˈskruːpjʊləs]

(a.) 多虑的；谨慎的，正直的

The judge was **scrupulous** in his decision to award the plaintiff with a $2,000 settlement.

unwitting
[ʌnˈwɪtɪŋ]

(a.) 不知情的；无知的

We should raise and lower the temperature in the classroom to observe how the **unwitting** subjects of our little experiment react.

fetching
[ˈfetʃɪŋ]

(a.)（尤指衣着方面）吸引人的

She looks so **fetching** when she wears that dress.

fastidious
[fæˈstɪdiəs]

(a.) 挑剔的，一丝不苟的；难以讨好的

To be a good editor, it is important to be very **fastidious**.

MP3-093

narcissism
[ˈnɑːsɪ(ə)sɪzəm]

(n.) 自我陶醉，自恋

The atmosphere of the supermodels' after show party was filled with **narcissism**.

派 narcissistic [ˌnɑːsɪˈsɪstɪk] (a.) 自恋的

tenacious
[tɪ(ə)ˈneɪʃəs]

(a.) 抓住不放的；固执的，不改其决定的

I wish that you wouldn't be so **tenacious** about these plans to go to Israel. We're going to go there someday. It doesn't need to be this year.

☑☐☐ 挑战单词 **Sophisticated vocabulary used in the IELTS Test**

fractious
[ˈfrækʃəs]

(a.) 易怒的，易抱怨的

The **fractious** housewife gave rise to many of the family problems.

wistful
[ˈwɪstfəl]

(a.) 惆怅的；念旧的

Sitting in her wheelchair watching the children playing, she became **wistful**, thinking once more about how she would never enjoy such freedom again.

solicitous
[səˈlɪsɪ(ə)təs]

(a.) 关切的，操心的

The **solicitous** mother always made sure that her children ate a healthy diet.

morose
[məˈrəʊs]

(a.) 闷闷不乐的

His **morose** mood is having a negative effect on me as well.

obdurate
[ˈɒbdʒʊrɪ(ə)t]

(a.) 执拗的，倔强的

He was **obdurate** in his decision despite the strong objections of his peers.

predilection
[ˌpriːdɪˈlekʃən]

(n.) 嗜好，偏爱
His **predilection** for insects was often the talk of his family.

propitiously
[prəˈpɪʃəsli]

(adv.) 适合地，有利地
His entrance into the company was **propitiously** timed; he can never set a foot wrong.

rapacious
[rəˈpeɪʃəs]

(a.) 贪婪的，贪得无厌的
The **rapacious** employee ensured by all means that he would be the top sales manager for the 3rd year running.

sagacious
[səˈgeɪʃəs]

(a.) 睿智的
The **sagacious** scholar wrote many books about morals and ideals.

supercilious
[ˌsuːpəˈsɪliəs]

(a.) 高傲的，目中无人的
Nothing is worse than having to tell **supercilious** people that they are wrong.

haughty
[ˈhɔːti]

(a.) 傲慢的
After that **haughty** glance she gave me, I find it hard to talk to her again.

provident
[ˈprɒvɪ(ə)dənt]

(a.) 顾及未来的，未雨绸缪的
The **provident** housewife has a pantry stocked with canned goods in case of an emergency.

querulous
[ˈkwerʊləs]

(a.)（尤指用恼人的语调）爱发牢骚的
His **querulous** wife is constantly nagging him about how much time he spends at his job.

volition

[vəˈlɪʃən]

(n.) 出于自己的意志或决定

Are you saying this of your own **volition** or is your mother pressuring you to make this statement?

Theme 15

MP3-094

Word Forms

☑☑☑ 高频单词 **Most frequently used vocabulary in the IELTS Test**

alternative
[ɔːl'tɜːnətɪv]

(n.) 可选择的方式，替代方案

We must consider every possible **alternative** before making this decision.

tremendous
[trɪ'mendəs]

(a.)（体积、数量或程度上）极大的，巨大的

The benefits of moving our factories from the United Kingdom to China are **tremendous**.

cynical
['sɪnɪkəl]

(a.) 挖苦的，嘲讽的；愤世嫉俗的

He is always so **cynical** about every suggestion that I make. It makes me not want to work for him anymore.

alongside
[əˌlɒŋ'saɪd]

(prep.) 沿着，靠着；在…旁边

After my coworkers came **alongside** me with this plan, everything went much more smoothly.

unsurprisingly
[ˌʌnsə'praɪzɪŋli]

(adv.) 不令人感到意外地，不足为奇地

Unsurprisingly, after the patient took more herbal medicine, his cold became much better.

permanently
['pɜːmənəntli]

(adv.) 不变地；恒久地

This solution will not fix the problem **permanently**. It will only provide a temporary solution.

MP3-095

considerably
[kən'sɪdərəbli]

(adv.) 非常；**相当大地，很大程度地**

My chances of getting into Harvard increased **considerably** after my professor wrote me that excellent letter of recommendation.

consequently
['kɒnsɪ(ə)kwəntli]

(adv.) **因此，所以**

He has a hard time hearing and **consequently** his family always yells when they want to talk to him.

intrusive
[ɪn'truːsɪv]

(a.) 强制的；侵入的；**打扰的**

I considered his **intrusive** questions about the financial condition of my family an invasion of my privacy.

obviously
['ɒbviəsli]

(adv.) **明显地，显而易见地**

The economy **obviously** suffers after natural disasters strike.

perplexed
[pə'plekst]

(a.) **困惑的**；不知所措的，混乱的

Even though the teacher patiently explained the grammar point a number of times, the students were still **perplexed**.

manifest
['mænɪ(ə)fest]

(v.) 以行动表示或证明；**显现，表现**

SARS first **manifests** itself as a high fever and coughs.

passionately
['pæʃənɪ(ə)tli]

(adv.) 热情地；**热烈激昂地**

The lawyer argued for his case **passionately** but ultimately lost because his reasoning had no logic.

reckless
['rekləs]

(a.) **不顾危险的，鲁莽不智的**

Driving after drinking is **reckless** behaviour.

oddly
[ˈɒdli]

(adv.) 奇怪地；古怪地

Oddly enough, the only professor at this school with an MBA degree works in the Department of Sociology.

unlikely
[ʌnˈlaɪkli]

(a.) 不大可能的

Because of the changes in the American economy and immigration policies after 9/11, it is **unlikely** that I will go there to get my PhD.

oppose
[əˈpəʊz]

(v.) 反对

I'm not **opposed** to you taking a vacation at Christmas. I just feel that it will be inconvenient considering that we will probably have more customers during that time.

priority
[praɪˈɒrɪ(ə)ti]

(n.) 优先考虑的事，最重要的事；优先（权）

Your first **priority** in a romantic relationship should not be what you can get from the other person, but rather what you can do for that person.

symbolise
[ˈsɪmbəlaɪz]

(v.) 象征；以符号代表

The government officials hope that constructing the world's tallest building will **symbolise** economic recovery after the destruction caused by the revolution.

defeat
[dɪˈfiːt]

(v.) 击败，战胜；使…破灭或失败

Opposition parties **defeated** the Labour Welsh Assembly Government in a debate on university tuition fees.

recognisable
[ˈrekəgnaɪzəbəl]

(a.) 易于辨认的

The skyscraper 101 is an easily **recognisable** landmark on the Taipei skyline as it is the second tallest building in the world.

MP3-096

attempt
[ə'tempt]

(v.) (n.) 企图，尝试

Don't even **attempt** to answer this question. It is way too difficult for you.

prolong
[prə'lɒŋ]

(v.) 延长，延伸；拖延

The more the construction of the building is **prolonged**, the more money we are going to lose on our investment.

craze
[kreɪz]

(n.) （一时的）狂热，风潮

The latest fashion **craze** in Europe has been girls wearing short skirts.

pathetic
[pə'θetɪk]

(a.) 可怜的；悲哀的

I can't believe you graduated from Cambridge and can't find a job. That is absolutely **pathetic**.

conceivable
[kən'siːvəbəl]

(a.) 可信的；可想象的；可能的

There is no **conceivable** reason for me to date you.

occasionally
[ə'keɪʒənəli]

(adv.) 偶尔

Occasionally I like to cook Western style food but most of the time I just eat Chinese.

factual
['fæktʃʊəl]

(a.) 真实的，（根据）事实的

We do not have any **factual** evidence that UFOs actually exist.

abide
[ə'baɪd]

(v.) 遵守；居留，停留

If citizens don't **abide** by the rules of society, they will be arrested by the police.

interfere
[ˌɪntə'fɪə]

(v.) 干涉；**妨害，扰乱**

Please don't **interfere** when I'm working; this job requires my full attention.

suspicious
[sə'spɪʃəs]

(a.) **可疑的，令人怀疑的**

His reasoning behind the car accident was very **suspicious**. I think it might actually be his fault after all.

exotic
[ɪg'zɒtɪk]

(a.) **具有异国风情的；**外来的

The flora in Taiwan is **exotic** to many Western tourists.

immense
[ɪ'mens]

(a.) **巨大的；**无边无际的

I'm afraid that this task gives me more responsibility than I can handle. I feel like I have this **immense** burden on my shoulders.

appeal
[ə'piːl]

(n.) 吸引；诉求；**恳求** (v.) **上诉；**恳求

On the basis of his **appeal**, I changed my mind about this plan and decided not to go forward with it.

The lawyer decided to **appeal** their case to the next higher court when the judge handed down an unfavourable decision.

subliminal
[sʌb'lɪmɪnəl]

(a.) 潜意识的；（广告或讯息）**间接的**

A long time ago movie theatres used to put **subliminal** messages into movies to try and make customers buy popcorn. I don't know if it actually worked though.

manipulate
[mə'nɪpjʊleɪt]

(v.) **操纵，控制；**影响

University scientific researchers are often put under pressure to **manipulate** the results to suit their sponsors.

MP3-097

revolutionise
[ˌrevəˈluːʃənaɪz]

(v.) 使产生根本性的巨大变革，彻底改变

If you really want to **revolutionise** this business, you have to think of something that nobody else has thought of yet.

virtual
[ˈvɜːtʃuəl]

(a.) 实际上的，实质上的

During the strike the factory was in a **virtual** state of shutdown.

initial
[ɪˈnɪʃəl]

(a.) 最初的，开始的 (n.) 姓名的第一个字母

My **initial** response to his comment was to laugh but then I realised that he was being serious.

reliable
[rɪˈlaɪəbəl]

(a.) 可靠的，可信赖的

The only **reliable** method of public transportation in my city is the bus.

accumulate
[əˈkjuːmjʊleɪt]

(v.)（经过较长的时间）累积，增加

The longer you work at this company, the more vacation days you will **accumulate**.

contagious
[kənˈteɪdʒəs]

(a.) 传染性的；（指情绪、感觉方面）有感染力的

Her laughter is **contagious**. As soon as she starts laughing, everybody else does too.

favourable
[ˈfeɪvərəbəl]

(a.) 令人高兴的；有帮助的

The only possible **favourable** result from this action is that people will have heard of our company's name.

ample
[ˈæmpəl]

(a.) 充足的；广阔的

Living with three other British people gives me **ample** opportunity to practise my English.

numerous
[ˈnjuːmərəs]

(a.) 极多的，数目众多的

There are **numerous** places to study English in Taipei but not many of them provide quality education.

burial
[ˈberɪəl]

(n.) 葬礼；埋葬

After attending the **burial**, it was impossible for him to do anything enjoyable for the rest of the day.

intrigue
[ˈɪntriːg]

(n.) 诡计；（对于较神秘或奇特事件的）兴趣

If it were not for the sense of **intrigue** that I felt in this subject, I would have dropped the class.

lavish
[ˈlævɪʃ]

(v.) 挥霍，花费；给予（金钱、赞美等）(a.) 大量的，挥霍的

The parents **lavished** so much praise on their children when they were young that they ended up spoiled.

fearsome
[ˈfɪəsəm]

(a.) 可怕的，惊人的

The chancellor remains a driven man with a **fearsome** capacity for work.

disintegrate
[dɪsˈɪntɪ(ə)greɪt]

(v.) 使分裂；崩溃，瓦解

After suffering four losses in a row, the team's morale **disintegrated**.

elaborate
[ɪˈlæbərɪ(ə)t]

(a.) 详尽的 (v.) 详加解释、说明

You don't need to give me such an **elaborate** explanation of what you were doing when you could simply say that you were out.

demonstrate
[ˈdemənstreɪt]

(v.) 证明；示范

I simply don't understand how to do this. Can you please **demonstrate** it for me?

MP3-098

eliminate
[ɪ'lɪmɪ(ə)neɪt]

(v.) 除去，剔除，淘汰

I cannot **eliminate** other job opportunities until I know for sure that Disney will hire me.

vigorous
['vɪgərəs]

(a.) 精力充沛的，健康有活力的

As well as dieting, **vigorous** exercise is another way to help you lose weight.

alter
['ɔːltə]

(v.) 改变；修改（衣服等）

The hurricane **altered** our plans to go to the beach for a picnic.

resemble
[rɪ'zembl]

(v.) 像，相似

Whenever he gets angry, I see just how much he **resembles** his father.

identical
[aɪ'dentɪkəl]

(a.) 完全相同的，非常相似的

That store is absolutely **identical** to the one that was there before. They just changed the name.

restore
[rɪ'stɔː]

(v.) 恢复；重建，修复

If we get eight hours of sleep, our bodies' energy will be **restored**.

voluntarily
['vɒləntərɪ(ə)li]

(adv.) 自愿地，自动地

He does not **voluntarily** express his feelings about the relationship between China and Japan.

drastically
['dræstɪkli]

(adv.) 彻底而突然地

The percentage of people who supported the Labour candidate fell **drastically** after the debate with his opponent.

facilitate
[fə′sɪlɪ(ə)teɪt]

(v.) 使容易；**促进**

The two businessmen were so angry at each other that they needed someone else to **facilitate** the meeting.

sabotage
[′sæbətɑːʒ]

(v.) **暗中破坏**

She is trying to **sabotage** their relationship by telling them lies about each other.

aggressive
[ə′gresɪv]

(a.) 挑衅的；**侵略的；**积极的

The **aggressive** way in which Bush conducted foreign policy caused other countries' citizens to dislike America.

coherent
[kəʊ′hɪərənt]

(a.) 一致的，协调的；**条理清楚的**

When I wake up in the morning, it is not possible for me to say anything **coherent**.

excessive
[ɪk′sesɪv]

(a.) **过多的，极度的**

The amount of money you spent on that watch was **excessive**. I don't understand why you couldn't buy a cheaper one.

trigger
[′trɪgə]

(v.) **引发；**扣扳机

Her comment about his ex-girlfriend was what **triggered** the breaking up of their relationship.

dynamic
[daɪ′næmɪk]

(a.) 力学的；**有活力的，朝气蓬勃的**

His personality is very **dynamic**. When he is at a party, everybody wants to be around him.

typical
[′tɪpɪkəl]

(a.) **典型的；**象征的，有代表性的

A **typical** day at work for many Koreans starts early in the morning and lasts all day.

MP3-099

ethnic
[ˈeθnɪk]

(a.) 种族的；**异国的**
My favourite kind of **ethnic** food is Mexican.

decisive
[dɪˈsaɪsɪv]

(a.) 决定性的；**坚决的，果断的**
His decision to resign from his position in the office was quite **decisive**. He actually left that very same day.

exuberant
[ɪɡˈzjuːbərənt]

(a.) **（人）精力充沛的；**（植物）生长繁茂的
Her attitude towards every situation is always **exuberant**. I don't know how she manages to have that much energy.

predominate
[prɪˈdɒmɪ(ə)neɪt]

(v.) 支配；**主导；**占优势
People with a liberal ideology **predominate** at that newspaper, hence most of their articles tend to slant to the left.

convey
[kənˈveɪ]

(v.) 运送；**传达**
It was hard for her to **convey** her views on that serious issue in such a short amount of time.

evoke
[ɪˈvəʊk]

(v.) **引起；**使忆起
I don't know why he always **evokes** such anger in me. I guess his personality is just really irritating.

edible
[ˈedɪ(ə)bl]

(a.) **可食用的**
Most Westerners don't consider raw eggs **edible** but people from other cultures eat them that way.

penetrate
[ˈpenɪ(ə)treɪt]

(v.) **看穿；**洞察；刺破
The look that she gave me felt as if it were **penetrating** into my very soul.

mimic
[ˈmɪmɪk]

(v.) 模仿

The best way to learn a proper British accent is to **mimic** the way they speak.

skeptical
[ˈskeptɪkl]

(a.) 怀疑的，多疑的，不相信的

The reason that I am **skeptical** about the promises that you give me is that you tend to not tell me the complete truth.

shed
[ʃed]

(v.) 释出；落下；摆脱；散发

His speech **shed** some light on a medical condition that has been puzzling researchers for many years.

搭 shed light on 阐明

surface
[ˈsɜːfɪ(ə)s]

(n.) 表面；外观 (v.) 浮出水面；出现

On the **surface** it may look as if she is fine, but actually her parents are going through a divorce right now.

It is dangerous for submarines to **surface** because they are then in danger of being seen.

imminent
[ˈɪmɪ(ə)nənt]

(a.) 即将发生的，逼近的

The closure of a number of post offices in the West Midlands is **imminent** due to the restructuring and modernisation programme.

precarious
[prɪˈkeəriəs]

(a.) 不稳固的；不确定的

Because of the typhoon, the branches of that tree are in a **precarious** position.

improbable
[ɪmˈprɒbəbəl]

(a.) 不太可能发生的；未必是事实的

It is **improbable** that they will ever be able to have children.

MP3-100

prevail
[prɪ'veɪl]

(v.) 占优势，战胜；流行，普及

He **prevailed** against all odds to win a seat in parliament.

As long as the people insist on not using condoms, AIDS will continue to **prevail**.

negligent
['neglɪdʒənt]

(a.) 疏忽的，大意的

The doctor was sued for his **negligent** behaviour in failing to inform his patient of the test results.

habitually
[hə'bɪtʃuəli]

(adv.) 习惯性地

He smokes **habitually**. He lights up on the hour.

day-to-day
[deɪ tə deɪ]

(a.) 每天的，日常的

My **day-to-day** schedule consists of school in the morning, a part-time job in the afternoon and studying in the evening.

remarkable
[rɪ'mɑːkəbəl]

(a.) 了不起的，杰出的；特别有趣而引人注目的

The event yesterday was **remarkable** because it was the first time that Jews and Protestants in Carlsburg sponsored an event together.

radical
['rædɪkəl]

(a.) 激进的，极端的

My professor's ideology is very **radical**. He believes in socialism so strongly that I wonder sometimes if he is actually a communist.

realistic
[ˌrɪə'lɪstɪk]

(a.) 实际的，现实的

The expectations that you have for me are simply not **realistic**. There is no way that I can fulfil them.

utilise
[ˈjuːtɪ(ə)laɪz]

(v.) 利用

This software is best **utilised** in accounting applications.

enhance
[ɪnˈhɑːns]

(v.) 提升（品质），加强

There are many products out there that claim to **enhance** a woman's beauty but I think that most of them are useless.

qualitative
[ˈkwɒlɪ(ə)tətɪv]

(a.) 质的；品质上的

Qualitative research is becoming more important than quantitative in the social sciences.

contemplate
[ˈkɒntəmpleɪt]

(v.) 深思；打算（未来想做的事或决定）

The reason that Tim chose to major in philosophy is because he likes to **contemplate** the meaning of things.

neutral
[ˈnjuːtrəl]

(a.) 中立的；（声音、表情）不带感情的，没有意见的

There are not very many people who have **neutral** opinions about the topic of gay marriages.

bond
[bɒnd]

(n.) 情感上的紧密结合；契约，债券

The **bond** between mother and child is said to be one of the most precious there is.

scope
[skəʊp]

(n.) 范围；机会；规模

The **scope** of this problem is larger than we originally anticipated.

ultimately
[ˈʌltɪ(ə)mɪ(ə)tli]

(adv.) 最终

I **ultimately** hope to become fluent in Chinese.

MP3-101

reinforce
[ˌriːɪ(ə)n'fɔːs]

(v.) 强化；支持，加强

The fact that English is becoming a more common language **reinforces** my argument that the world is increasingly becoming more connected.

refine
[rɪ'faɪn]

(v.) 改善（较细微的事物）；使优雅；使纯净

Her time with her grandparents in England **refined** her manners considerably.

behalf
[bɪ'hɑːf]

(n.) 代表

Can you ask him a favour on my **behalf**?

搭 on sb's behalf 代表某人

supplementary
[ˌsʌplɪ(ə)'mentəri]

(a.) 补充的

My math level is not high enough to enter college so I need to go to a private school to receive **supplementary** education.

preliminary
[prɪ'lɪmɪ(ə)nəri]

(a.) 初步的，开端的

Before we can begin this class, I have a few **preliminary** matters to talk about.

forthcoming
[ˌfɔːθ'kʌmɪŋ]

(a.) 愿意（帮忙或提供讯息）的；即将到来的

Peace between Palestinians and Israelis will be easier to attain if both sides are **forthcoming** about their needs, intentions and goals.

persistent
[pə'sɪstənt]

(a.) 持续的；坚持的

I would have never woken up if not for the **persistent** ringing of my alarm clock.

so-called
[səʊ kɔːld]

(a.) 所谓的（尤指以不以为然的态度形容某人的称谓或关系）

His **so-called** girlfriend actually broke up with him three months ago.

reassuring
[ˌriːəˈʃʊərɪŋ]

(a.)（使）安心的，安抚的

My manager's praise is very **reassuring** to me. She is always encouraging me to do better.

The nurse's **reassuring** utterances helped to reduce the child's fears and she soon fell asleep.

hazardous
[ˈhæzədəs]

(a.) 危险的，危害的

Drinking alcohol and smoking cigarettes are very **hazardous** to your health.

endanger
[ɪnˈdeɪndʒə^{r}]

(v.) 危害，使…有危险

Do not **endanger** children by placing them within reach of poisonous chemicals.

risk
[rɪsk]

(v.) 冒着…的危险

I don't smoke because I am not willing to **risk** my health or that of my unborn child.

courtesy
[ˈkɜːtɪ(ə)si]

(n.) 有礼的举止，礼貌

While I was in the hospital, he did not even have the **courtesy** to pay me a visit.

coincidental
[kəʊˌɪnsɪ(ə)ˈdentl]

(a.) 巧合的

My chance meeting with him on the street was not **coincidental**—he had planned to run into me.

MP3-102

turbulent
[ˈtɜːbjʊlənt]

(a.) 狂乱的；动荡不安的

Due to the **turbulent** social and political climate in South Africa, hospitals in the poorer townships are being flooded with victims of violence.

irreplaceable
[ˌɪrɪˈpleɪsəbəl]

(a.) 无法取代的

Nurse Sloane knows so much about our clinic that she is **irreplaceable**. We'll have to give her a pay raise so she doesn't leave.

breakthrough
[ˈbreɪkθruː]

(n.) 突破，重大进展

The discovery of the antibiotic properties of penicillin was a **breakthrough** for medicine, enabling a whole new realm of possibilities.

applied
[əˈplaɪd]

(a.) 应用的，实用的

After completing his MA in **Applied** Linguistics, he went overseas to forge ahead with his career in the ELT (English Language Teaching) industry.

envisage
[ɪnˈvɪzɪdʒ]

(v.) 设想；可预见

Due to the increased incidence of serious flu this year, it's **envisaged** that free flu shots will be provided to the general public next year.

integrated
[ˈɪntrɪ(ə)greɪtɪ(ə)d]

(a.) 融入的，整合的

The basic component of microelectronics is **integrated** circuits.

搭 integrated circuit 集成电路

nonetheless
[ˌnʌnðəˈles]

(adv.) 虽然如此，但是

You have made a strong recovery over the past week, **nonetheless**, we will need to keep you in hospital for further observation for at least two more weeks.

privileged
[ˈprɪvɪ(ə)lɪdʒd]

(a.) 享有特权的

Scientific philosophers have grave concerns that genetically engineered babies may only be available to the **privileged** classes who have the money to pay for one.

extraordinary
[ɪkˈstrɔːdənəri]

(a.) 惊人的，非凡的；非常特别的

The patient's full recovery from cancer by changing to a fully organic diet was **extraordinary**.

absurd
[əbˈsɜːd]

(a.) 荒谬的

It would be **absurd** to suggest that the prescription of drugs was the only method to consider in the treatment of disease.

overshadow
[ˌəʊvəˈʃædəʊ]

(v.) 给…蒙上阴影，使…黯然失色

When working as a doctor in war-torn countries, it is important not to let small successes be **overshadowed** by the huge task looming ahead of you.

fluctuate
[ˈflʌktʃueɪt]

(v.) 波动，起伏

The number of first-year medical students has been **fluctuating** from year to year due to changing government policies regarding hospitals.

inevitable
[ɪˈnevɪ(ə)təbəl]

(a.) 无法避免的；必然的

Although death will always be **inevitable**, in the near future we will be able to delay it for many years.

MP3-103

striking
[ˈstraɪkɪŋ]

(a.) 显著的，惊人的

The difference between the number of students using email now and that of five years ago is **striking**.

agitation
[ˌædʒɪ(ə)ˈteɪʃən]

(n.) 忧虑不安；紧张情势

The patient's father was in a state of high **agitation** after hearing that his daughter's illness might be incurable.

coating
[ˈkəʊtɪŋ]

(n.) 外层（涂料）；覆盖层

The **coating** on these pills tastes good so that parents won't have trouble administering them to their children.

install
[ɪnˈstɔːl]

(v.) 安装，架设；安顿

Once this heart rate monitor is **installed**, we are going to start using it on the patients straight away.

insulate
[ˈɪnsjʊleɪt]

(v.) 使绝缘，使隔离（冷，热，噪音，电等）

Households which **insulate** their homes will receive a government rebate.

miniature
[ˈmɪnɪ(ə)tʃəʳ]

(a.) 缩影的；小规模的，微型的

In the future, **miniature** robots will be able to travel through our arteries to repair our bodies.

proportionate
[prəˈpɔːʃənɪ(ə)t]

(a.) 成比例的；匀称的

Your ideal weight is **proportionate** not only to your height, but also to the size and density of your bones.

cyclic
[ˈsaɪklɪk]

(a.) 循环的，周期性的

Because of the **cyclic** nature of their reproductive system, women are able to eliminate toxins from their body on a regular basis.

diversity
[daɪˈvɜːsɪ(ə)ti]

(n.) 变化，多样性

There are fears that human cloning will eventually lead to the loss of genetic **diversity** in our species as unwanted characteristics are eradicated.

crucial
[ˈkruːʃəl]

(a.) 决定性的；重要的

If you want to recover from heart disease, it is **crucial** that you undertake a programme of moderate cardiovascular exercise for two hours every day.

reluctant
[rɪˈlʌktənt]

(a.) 不情愿的

Most doctors are **reluctant** to prescribe sleeping pills unless there is an urgent need for them as they do not cure the root of the problem.

unprecedented
[ʌnˈpresɪ(ə)dentɪ(ə)d]

(a.) 前所未有的；史无前例的

We are having **unprecedented** success with the new asthma drug and hope it will be available worldwide in the near future.

speculate
[ˈspekjʊleɪt]

(v.) 思索，沉思；推测；做投机买卖

The reporter **speculated** about whether the new government would indeed increase education funding as it had promised in its election campaign.

estimate
[ˈestɪ(ə)meɪt]

(v.) 估计；估价；预估

A preview of the construction plans will help the builders **estimate** an approximate cost for the project.

redundant
[rɪˈdʌndənt]

(a.) 多余的；〈英〉解雇的，失业的

The discovery and invention of new antibiotics have helped to render penicillin **redundant** despite its importance in history.

MP3-104

extravagant
[ɪkˈstrævəgənt]

(a.) 挥霍的，铺张的；过度的

The decorations at our university's commencement ceremonies are very **extravagant**.

tendency
[ˈtendənsi]

(n.) 倾向；趋势

If your child has a **tendency** to avoid social interaction with other children and difficulty learning language skills, he could be autistic.

attribute
[əˈtrɪbjuːt]

(v.) 归因于

The man's death was **attributed** to natural causes.

compatible
[kəmˈpætɪ(ə)bəl]

(a.) 可相容的；可共处的

The great advantage of the O blood type is that it is **compatible** with most other types in blood transfusions.

cultivate
[ˈkʌltɪ(ə)veɪt]

(v.) 耕作，栽培；养殖，培养

The bacteria from the swabs are **cultivated** in the laboratory in order to identify the patient's disease.

enthusiastic
[ɪnˌθjuːziˈæstɪk]

(a.) 热情的，充满热忱的

The students at this college are all very **enthusiastic** about the subjects they are learning.

keen
[kiːn]

(a.) 热衷的；激烈的；敏锐的

I am very **keen** on continuing with the plan that we originally made.

fabulous
[ˈfæbjʊləs]

(a.) 极好的，惊人的

These herbs are **fabulous** at assisting weight loss. My sister has lost four kilogrammes in two weeks.

arise
[ə'raɪz]

(v.) 出现，发生；升起

Health problems can **arise** as a result of stress combined with inadequate nutrition, both of which are due to overwork.

coincide
[ˌkəʊɪ(ə)n'saɪd]

(v.) 同时发生；一致，相符

If the results of the two independent studies **coincide** and are positive, the medical establishment will consider taking the Atkins diet more seriously.

incident
['ɪnsɪ(ə)dənt]

(n.) 事件；（意外的）插曲或事故

The bypass operation was completed without **incident** and the Prime Minister is now recovering in hospital.

drastic
['dræstɪk]

(a.) 极端的，激烈的

In emergency war situations, **drastic** measures such as amputation of limbs are necessary at times.

straightforward
[ˌstreɪt'fɔːwəd]

(a.) 简单易懂的，直截了当的；诚实的

The CEO of this company likes all of his questions to be answered in a **straightforward** manner.

subsidiary
[səb'sɪdiəri]

(a.) 次要的，辅助的；附属的

There are doctors who believe that diet plays only a **subsidiary** role in the onset of cancer and that genetics accounts for 85% of the risk factors.

passive
['pæsɪv]

(a.) 被动的，消极的

Passive smoking is even more dangerous than that engaged in by the smoker because none of the toxins are filtered out of the burning end of the cigarette.

搭 passive smoking 吸二手烟

MP3-105

lapse
[læps]

(v.)（契约）终止；（时间）流逝；**陷入**

The cancer patient finally **lapsed** into a coma, giving him relief from his agony.

harmonise
[ˈhɑːmənaɪz]

(v.) **使调和，使和谐**

If human beings can **harmonise** their lifestyles with nature, their health will improve in many ways.

concrete
[ˈkɒŋkriːt]

(a.) **具体的；**有形的，实在的

Forensic scientists were able to provide **concrete** evidence of the attacker's identity.

arouse
[əˈraʊz]

(v.) 唤起，引起；**激发**

Taking a class in investments **aroused** my interest in business as a whole.

compulsive
[kəmˈpʌlsɪv]

(a.) 强制的；**强迫性的，无法控制或停止的**

He has been fighting a **compulsive** addiction to smoking for two years.

differentiate
[ˌdɪfəˈrenʃieɪt]

(v.) **区分**

It is important to **differentiate** between the symptoms of different strains of hepatitis in order to take appropriate action in curing the disease.

substantiate
[səbˈstænʃieɪt]

(v.) **证明，证实**

The company appears to be unable to **substantiate** their claims as to the effectiveness of the herbal medicine. I think it should be taken off the shelves.

admonish
[əd′mɒnɪʃ]

(v.) 告诫，责备

The professor **admonished** the students for being late to class.

allege
[ə′ledʒ]

(v.)（没有证据的）指控，断言，主张

The teacher **alleged** that the student had cheated in the exam, but could not prove it.

allocate
[′æləkeɪt]

(v.) 拨出，分配

The government should **allocate** more of its health funding to the promotion of exercise to prevent disease.

ambiguous
[æm′bɪgjuəs]

(a.) 暧昧的，不明确的

When I asked my sister about her first date last night, her answer was rather **ambiguous**. I hope there's nothing wrong that she's not telling me.

accessible
[ək′sesɪ(ə)bəl]

(a.) 易达到的，易取得的；易了解的

The government should subsidise gene therapy to make it **accessible** to all and not just the wealthy.

considerable
[kən′sɪdərəbəl]

(a.) 相当多的，相当大的；重要的

After spending **considerable** time promoting this product, it is disappointing to see it fail.

apprehensive
[ˌæprɪ′hensɪv]

(a.) 担忧的，不安的

After the terrible car accident, the driver was quite **apprehensive** about getting into a car again.

MP3-106

convert
[kən'vɜːt]

(v.) 改变；转换，使改变信仰

The government decided to **convert** the old hospital into a large nursing home.

definitive
[dɪ'fɪnɪ(ə)tɪv]

(a.) 权威的；最后的

Stodgeson and Wickham is the **definitive** reference for the treatment of tropical diseases today; there's none better.

obscure
[əb'skjʊə^r]

(a.) 难理解的；不清楚的；鲜为人知的

His Arabic is very good, but sometimes he will know the most **obscure** word, while not understanding some simple sentences.

painstaking
['peɪnzˌteɪkɪŋ]

(a.) 非常用心、仔细的；煞费苦心的

The **painstaking** research into cures for cancer promises to have many helpful future applications.

profound
[prə'faʊnd]

(a.) 深切的，完全的

After he took painting classes, the psychiatrist observed a **profound** improvement in the patient's mental health.

toss-up
[tɒs ʌp]

(n.) 输赢各半、平分秋色的状况

It's a **toss-up** between who will be nominated as the new director. It'll be either Helen Jones or Richard Keats.

commute
[kə'mjuːt]

(v.) 往来，通勤

Nurses should not have to **commute** to work due to the irregular hours of shifts and the stressful demands of the job. Therefore, the hospital provides accommodation for them.

☑☑☐ 精选单词 **Specialised vocabulary used in the IELTS Test**

comparatively
[kəmˈpærətɪ(ə)vli]

(adv.) **比较地；**有点，稍微

This plan has **comparatively** no advantage over the other one.

wholesome
[ˈhəʊlsəm]

(a.) **有益的；**促进健康的

The movies that Disney makes are always very **wholesome**.

fictitious
[fɪkˈtɪʃəs]

(a.) **虚构的，编造的；**假的

His claim to this land's property rights is absolutely **fictitious**. There is no way that his ancestors lived here previously.

impair
[ɪmˈpeə^r]

(v.) **受损，减弱**

His ability to hear is **impaired** from years of working in the coal mines.

acclaim
[əˈkleɪm]

(v.) **称赞，喝彩，受到好评**

The latest art show at the museum has been widely **acclaimed** by a variety of newspapers.

remit
[rɪˈmɪt]

(v.) **汇款；**赦免，免除

I will **remit** the payment to you as soon as I receive my paycheque.

enlightening
[ɪnˈlaɪtnɪŋ]

(a.) **启发的，给予知识的**

The things he told me about America's policies in Iraq were very **enlightening**.

MP3-107

embed
[ɪm'bed]

(v.) 埋入；**深留；**使铭记于心

Racism is so deeply **embedded** in society that people prefer to ignore it by thinking that it doesn't exist anymore.

emergent
[ɪ'mɜːdʒənt]

(a.) 初萌生的；**新兴起的**

Emergent technologies tend to be very expensive.

cumulative
['kjuːmjʊlətɪv]

(a.) **累积的，一点一滴增加的**

Working long hours has a **cumulative** negative effect on one's health.

embellish
[ɪm'belɪʃ]

(v.) 装饰；**添加，润色**

He likes to **embellish** his stories a lot so they end up only a watered-down version of the truth.

pervasive
[pə'veɪsɪv]

(a.) **处处可见的，普及的**

A sense of duty to one's elders is **pervasive** throughout Chinese culture.

unearth
[ʌn'ɜːθ]

(v.) 发现，揭晓；**挖掘**

Newspaper reports often **unearth** interesting information about famous people for their articles.

transitional
[træn'zɪʃənəl]

(a.) **过渡时期的；**改变期的

Many homeless people need to stay in a **transitional** shelter before being able to find a more permanent home.

conceptually
[kən'septʃuəli]

(adv.) **概念上地**

This idea makes sense **conceptually** but I'm not sure if it will work in reality.

well-stated
[wel ˈsteɪtɪ(ə)d]

(a.) 陈述完整的
Your point was very **well-stated** but I still don't agree with you.

reflective
[rɪˈflektɪv]

(a.) 反射的，反映的；深思熟虑的
When making a decision of that magnitude, it is good to be careful and **reflective**.

discernible
[dɪˈsɜːnəbl]

(a.) 可辨识的
The fact that he is from Brazil is barely **discernible** from his accent.

ominous
[ˈɒmɪ(ə)nəs]

(a.) 不祥的，险恶的
The clouds to the east look very **ominous**. We may be getting a thunderstorm soon.

downplay
[ˌdaʊnˈpleɪ]

(v.) 轻描淡写，刻意减轻其严重性、重要性
The Finance Minister tried to **downplay** the economic crisis at his press conference.

culminate
[ˈkʌlmɪ(ə)neɪt]

(v.) 达到高峰，以…作结
I hope that my career will **culminate** in my becoming the CEO of a large company.

dodgy
[ˈdɒdʒi]

(a.) 不诚实的，不可信赖的；困难、危险的
His **dodgy** behaviour made everybody worried that something was wrong with him.

menace
[ˈmenɪ(ə)s]

(n.) 威胁，危险 (v.) 威胁，恐吓
That criminal is a **menace** to society.

MP3-108

uncompromising
[ʌnˈkɒmprəmaɪzɪŋ]

(a.) 不妥协的，坚定的

A doctor must have an **uncompromising** sense of ethics where concerns for the patient's well-being totally override any interest in making money.

ponder
[ˈpɒndəʳ]

(v.) 深思，谨慎判断

After hearing the unusual description of the patient's symptoms, the doctors **pondered** their next move. Experience and intuition told them it would be one of the two conditions.

clumsy
[ˈklʌmzi]

(a.) 动作笨拙的，不灵巧的；粗心大意的

The **clumsy** manner in which he managed our investment fund caused us to lose a lot of money when the economy fell.

successive
[səkˈsesɪv]

(a.) 继续的，连接的；（职务）连任的

The Governor General has served five **successive** terms since leaving his post in the federal government.

conceptual
[kənˈseptʃuəl]

(a.) 概念的

This new method of physiotherapy for accident victims is only in its **conceptual** stage. There is a lot of work to be done in actually implementing it.

frugal
[ˈfruːgəl]

(a.) 简约的；（食物）少量简单的

It was found that farmers who ate **frugal** meals every day lived longer than the average person.

imprudent
[ɪmˈpruːdənt]

(a.) 不智的，欠考虑的

Imprudent use of sleeping pills can lead to long-term sleeping problems. Take them only when necessary.

feasible
[ˈfiːzɪ(ə)bəl]

(a.) 可行的；可能的，合理的

After looking at our income statements we decided that it was not **feasible** for us to buy a new car.

haphazard
[ˌhæpˈhæzəd]

(a.) 随意的，无计划或程序的

Some doctors prescribe antibiotics in a **haphazard** manner, thus risking the occurrence of more and more drug-resistant strains of serious diseases such as tuberculosis.

dicey
[ˈdaɪsi]

(a.) 不太确定的；有点危险的

Those vegetables look **dicey**. I wouldn't eat them.

arduous
[ˈɑːdjuəs]

(a.) 费力的，艰巨的

The task of writing down all the soldiers' details including the circumstances in which they were injured is an **arduous** one, but it will help doctors to learn more about the patterns of war injury.

feeble
[ˈfiːbəl]

(a.) 虚弱无力的；站不住脚的；不好的

The boss fired the employee because he had given too many **feeble** excuses for being late.

utter
[ˈʌtəʳ]

(v.) 发出（声音），说 (a.) 全然的，彻底的

After hearing the results of her tests, she did not **utter** a sound, such was her shock.

In Vietnam, army medical personnel had to carry out their duties as normal amidst the **utter** chaos of war.

outright
[ˈaʊtraɪt]

(a.) 完全的，彻底的 (adv.) 立即

The judge decided that he was the **outright** winner of the race.

MP3-109

rigid
[ˈrɪdʒɪ(ə)d]

(a.) 僵硬的；严格的，死板的

If you allow your back muscles to become too **rigid**, it can cause serious spinal problems, so it is important to stretch them regularly.

bumpy
[ˈbʌmpi]

(a.) 崎岖不平的，起伏不定的

The road to a better life may be **bumpy**, but it is worth it.

impel
[ɪmˈpel]

(v.) 驱策；促使

When I saw the sick, abused dog, I felt **impelled** to help her by taking her to the nearest veterinarian.

ambivalent
[æmˈbɪvələnt]

(a.) 怀有矛盾心情的，不能确定的

The director only responds to his wife's advice. To all others he is **ambivalent**.

allusive
[əˈluːsɪv]

(a.) 提及的；隐喻的，暗指的

The candidate's speech at the convention contained many **allusive** comments about his opponent's supposed inability to be a competent prime minister.

assiduous
[əˈsɪdjuəs]

(a.) 一丝不苟的；努力不懈的

His **assiduous** research into the effects of alcohol on the human body has led to many lives being saved.

belittle
[bɪˈlɪtl]

(v.) 蔑视，贬低

The conceited way in which the boss **belittles** his employees is very disconcerting.

cognitive
[ˈkɒgnɪ(ə)tɪv]

(a.) 认知的
The scientist's research into the **cognitive** capabilities of the human brain led to many new discoveries that may have medical application in the future.

conductive
[kənˈdʌktɪv]

(a.) **传导性的，导电的**
Steel is used in the body scanner because it is a **conductive** metal and the electrons can travel through it rapidly.

elusive
[ɪˈluːsɪv]

(a.) 难以捉摸的；**难以成就的**
His incredible work ethic comes from his belief that the more he works, the closer he will get to the **elusive** goal of becoming a company's CEO.

incessant
[ɪnˈsesənt]

(a.)（常指令人不悦的事）**不停的，没完没了的**
The **incessant** nature of his complaints is very aggravating to me.

nominal
[ˈnɒmɪ(ə)nəl]

(a.) **名义上的，有名无实的**
The director is the **nominal** head of the firm. In reality, the manager of each department makes most of the decisions.

prudent
[ˈpruːdənt]

(a.) **慎重的，谨慎的**
One of the major reasons that this company was able to prevent going into bankruptcy was because of the decisions made by our **prudent** Chief Financial Officer.

repudiate
[rɪˈpjuːdieɪt]

(v.) 拒绝接受；**驳斥，否认**
The Prime Minister **repudiated** the allegations put forward by the media about his personal life.

MP3-110

superficial
[ˌsuːpəˈfɪʃəl]

(a.) 表面（上）的，肤浅的；虚假的

Due to her **superficial** nature, I couldn't establish a solid friendship with her and really get to know how she thinks.

tacit
[ˈtæsɪ(ə)t]

(a.) 默许的，心照不宣的

She received his **tacit** agreement that he would give up gambling from his silence at her imploring request.

tangible
[ˈtændʒɪ(ə)bəl]

(a.) 具体的，实质的

To believe you, I need **tangible** evidence of what you are saying is true.

take the plunge
[teɪk ðə plʌndʒ]

(v.) 深思熟虑后决定冒险尝试

Although she did not relish the thought of receiving acupuncture, she decided to **take the plunge** as she had heard stories of its success in aiding weight loss.

fruitful
[ˈfruːtfəl]

(a.) 有收获的，有效的

The only way to know if the results of your proposal will be **fruitful** is to try it out.

myriad
[ˈmɪriəd]

(n.) 无数，大量

While there are a **myriad** of factors involved in the treatment of cancer, prevention is still better than cure.

☑☐☐ 挑战单词 **Sophisticated vocabulary used in the IELTS Test**

deleterious
[ˌdelɪ(ə)ˈtɪəriəs]

(a.) 有害的

Eating less meat will have no **deleterious** effect on your health.

befall
[bɪ'fɔːl]

(v.)（指不好的事或遭遇）发生，降临

This is the worst problem to **befall** me in the past ten years.

unfettered
[ʌn'fetəd]

(a.) 不受拘束或限制的，天马行空的

I want your **unfettered** opinion on this matter.

stout
[staʊt]

(a.) 胖的；粗壮的，结实的

As people get older and **stouter**, they must become more aware of their diet and the need to exercise to prevent heart disease.

sap
[sæp]

(n.) 汁液，树液

Native American doctors took the **sap** from certain trees to use in medicines.

vacuous
['vækjuəs]

(a.) 无意义的，空洞的

The Hollywood actor dismissed the **vacuous** question put forward by the reporter at the press conference.

fallacious
[fə'leɪʃəs]

(a.) 错误的，谬误的，不合理的

Some companies which advertise their products on television make **fallacious** claims that they can aid in weight reduction without the need to cut calories or exercise.

abhor
[əb'hɔːr]

(v.)（尤指道德方面）厌恶

I **abhor** the way children are used for labour purposes in some developing countries.

MP3-111

antithesis
[æn'tɪθɪ(ə)sɪ(ə)s]

(n.) 完全相反；对照

Professor Marlborough appears to be the **antithesis** of a murderer: warm, caring, and conversational. I can't believe he was convicted!

capricious
[kə'prɪʃəs]

(a.) 善变的，任性的

The child's **capricious** nature didn't make her a good student at school.

delude
[dɪ'luːd]

(v.) 误导，欺骗

Although positive thinking can be helpful, it is important not to **delude** yourself that recovery from such a serious disease is a certainty as this could lead to severe disappointment.

equivocal
[ɪ'kwɪvəkəl]

(a.) 含糊的；不确定的，模棱两可的

The result of this year's research into the human genome is of an **equivocal** nature. We are not yet sure what the potential applications will be.

flout
[flaʊt]

(v.) 蔑视，违抗

It's disturbing to think that some motorists still **flout** the drink-driving laws in this country.

specious
['spiːʃəs]

(a.) 华而不实的；似是而非的

Many advertisements contain **specious** arguments that some newly-found nutritional product will cause weight loss unaided.

IELTS

VOCABULARY FOCUS

写作高分重点词汇

Writing Task 1

图表分析常用词汇

v.= verb　a.= adjective　n.= noun　adv.= adverb

sth.= something　s.= subject　conj.= conjunction　phr.= phrase

A：重要句型

same 表示相同、类似的

* sth. is similar to sth.
* sth. is the same as sth.
* there is/are as many/much n. as sth.
* sth. is as a. as sth.
* sth. is not different from sth.
* sth. is just like sth.
* sth. is identical to sth.
* sth. is indistinguishable from sth.
* sth. is equal to sth.
* sth. has remained unchanged.
* sth. corresponds to sth.
* sth. is consistent with sth.
* sth. coincides with sth.

different 表示不同的

* sth. is different from sth.
* sth. is unlike sth.
* sth. varies from sth.
* sth. differs from sth.
* sth. contrasts with sth.
* sth. bears no relation to sth.
* sth. is a far cry from sth.

* there is a world of difference between sth. and sth.
* sth. is not as a. as sth.
* there is a striking disparity between sth. and sth.

amount 表示分量、数量多寡及改变

* the amount of n. (uncountable)
* the number of n. (countable)
* the percentage of n.
* the proportion of n.
* the level of n.
* the portion of n.
* the quantity of n.
* the volume of n.
* the total/sum of n.
* the rate of n.
* the ratio of n.
* the fraction of n.
* the extent of n.
* the incidence of n.
* sth. is half as much as sth.
* sth. is twice as much as sth.
* sth. is three times as much as sth.
* sth. is double that of sth.
* sth. is three times more than sth.

B：a. + n./v. + adv. 的规则与例句

dramatic + n.

There was a **dramatic increase** of $50 million in car sales between 1900 and 2000.

v. + dramatically

The number of cars leased **rose dramatically** throughout the decade.

a.	n./v.	adv.
minimal		minimally
slow		slowly
slight		slightly
steady	increase	steadily
gradual		gradually
dramatic		dramatically
steep		steeply
rapid		rapidly
sudden		suddenly
sharp	decrease	sharply
drastic		drastically
considerable		considerably
significant		significantly

其他与increase近似的单词与词组：

climb, double, escalate, explode, gain, grow, leap, multiply, quadruple, rise, rocket, soar, surge, triple, be at a peak, go through the roof, pick up, reach a peak, shoot up

其他与decrease近似的单词与词组：

decline, diminish, drop, dwindle, fall, plunge, reduce, slide, be at the lowest point, reach an all-time low, take a nosedive

C：必备实用单词

必备单词	词性	中文释义
while	conj.	而，然而
portion	n.	（一）部分
proportion	n.	容积，比率（常用于pie chart饼图）
occupy	v.	占，占了
occur	v.	发生
indicate	v.	指出
indicative	a.	指示
reach	v.	达到（常用于line graph曲线图）
gradual	a.	渐进的
drastically	adv.	彻底地
unstable	a.	不稳定的
stable	a.	不变的
constant	a.	不变的
considerably	adv.	相当多地
steeply	adv.	急剧地
dramatically	adv.	显著地
dip	v.	下陷，下降（形容曲线图中下降的部分）
illustrate	v.	图示，（以图）说明
all-time	a.	空前的
minimal	a.	最小的
figure	n.	数字；图
diminish	v.	减少，缩小
negligible	a.	微不足道的
exclusively	adv.	独占地，专门地
divide into	v.	分（割）成
attribute to	v.	归因于
tend to	v.	趋向于
divert ... away	v.	转向，转出
more likely	phr.	较可能是
as can be expected	phr.	可预期的
in ascending order	phr.	由下往上的顺序

Line Graph

曲线图

A

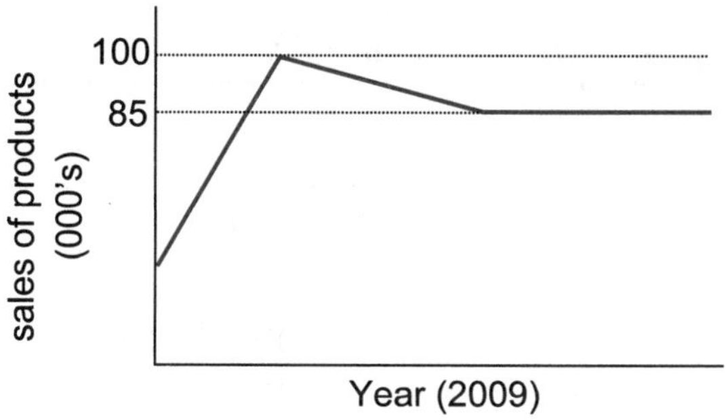

Sales of our products **increased sharply to reach a peak** of 100,000 units, after which sales **fell slightly** and then stabilised over the last few months at the **lower number** of 85,000 units.

B

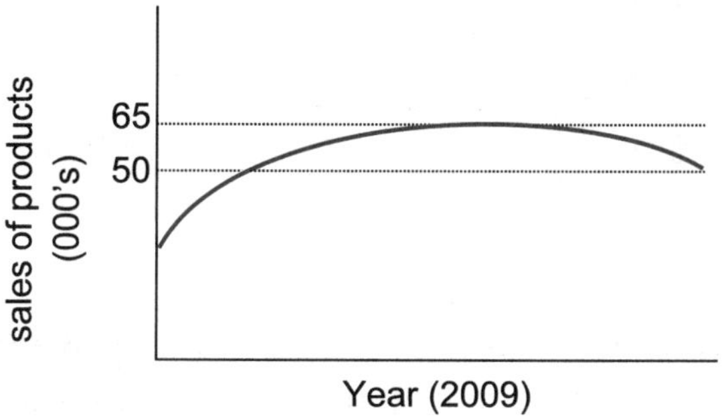

Sales of our products had been on a **gradual rise** before **reaching a plateau** of 65,000 units and then **falling slightly** to 50,000 units in the last few months.

C

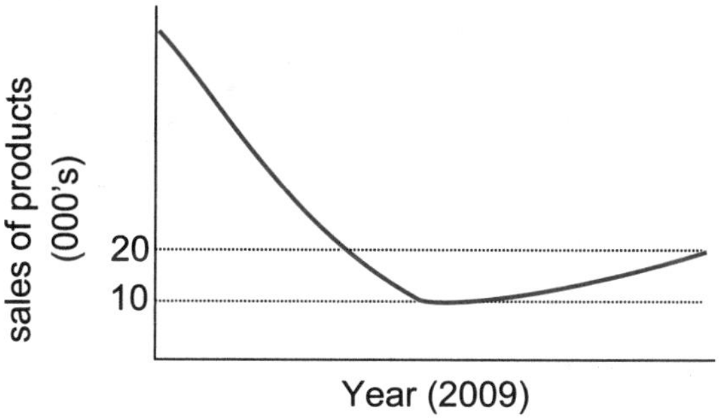

Sales of our products **had fallen drastically** during the first half of 2009 until finally **hitting a low point** of 10,000 units, after which sales **rose slightly** to 20,000 units.

D

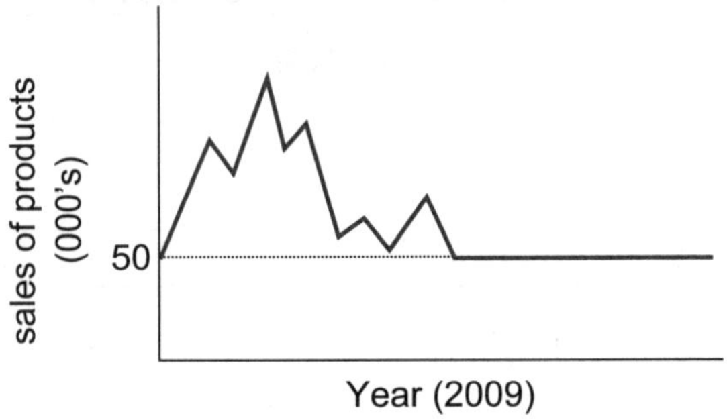

For the first half of 2009 , sales of our products were **relatively unstable**, especially compared to the last half of the year in which sales **remained constant** at 50,000 units sold per month.

E

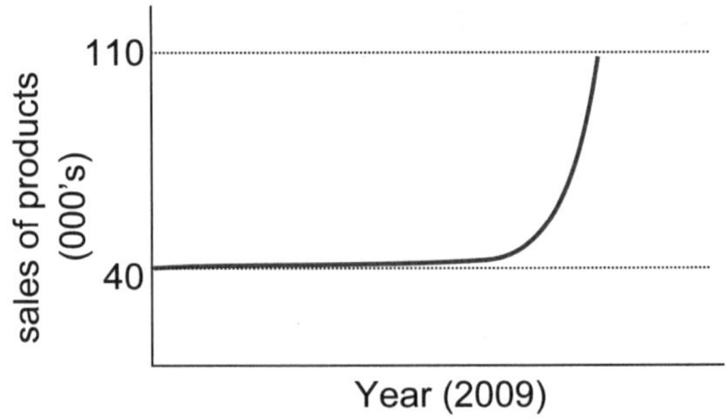

For the first three quarters, sales of our products **remained the same** at 40,000 units sold. It was only in the last quarter that sales **increased rapidly** to **an all-time high** of 110,000 units.

F

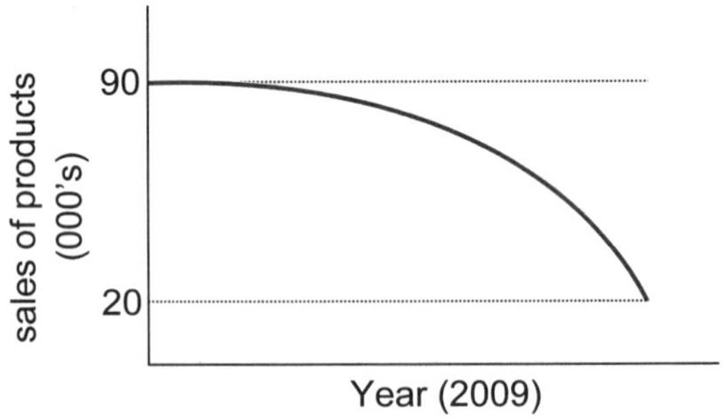

Sales of our products had been on a **steady decline** over the year, **dropping** from 90,000 units at the beginning of the year to 20,000 units at the close.

G

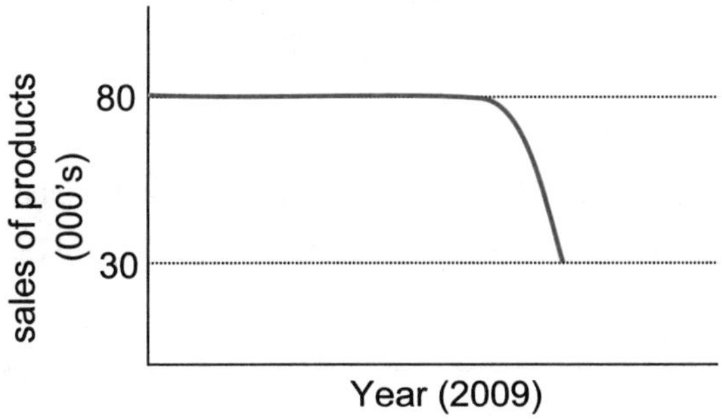

Sales of our products had **remained stable** at 80,000 units sold during the first nine months of the year until **dropping considerably** to 30,000 units sold in the final quarter.

H

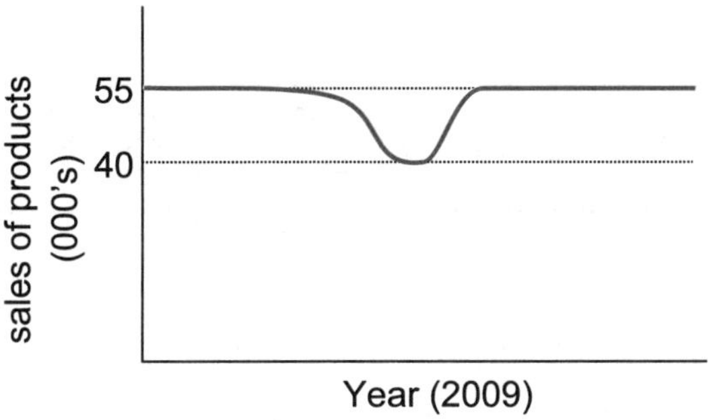

Sales of our products **dipped slightly** during the middle of 2009 , from 55,000 to 40,000 units sold. This dip **fully recovered** by the final quarter though, with final sales at 55,000 units sold.

Graph Chart

折线图

Government investment in the Arts in the past 25 years as indicated by the annual budget of the National Endowment for the Arts (NEA).

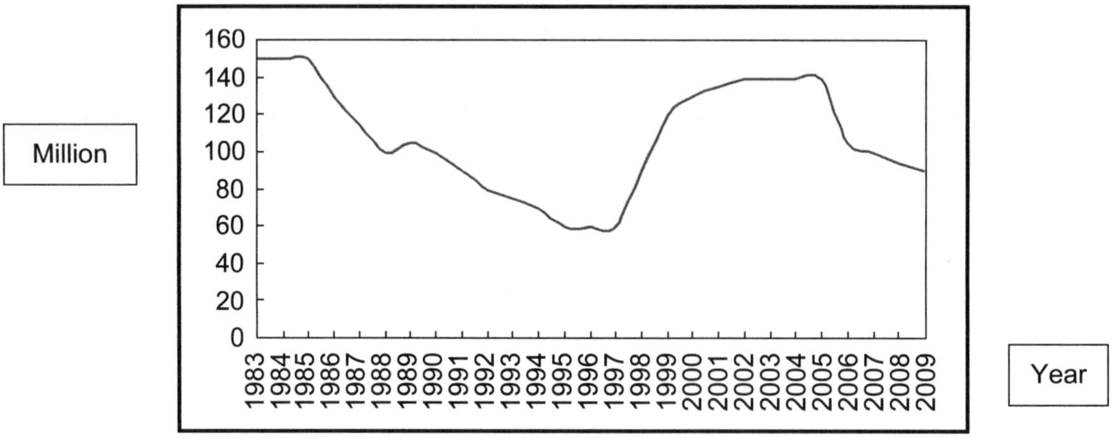

After starting **at a high** of $150 million in 1983, funding for the Arts **declined sharply** over the next 5 years to $100 million.

Following a **slight rise** of under $100 million in 1988, the trend further **decreased gradually** to **reach an all-time low** of $60 million in 1995.

There was **minimal change** between the years 1995 and 1997. There was a **dramatic increase** in funding from $60 million in 1997 to $140 million in 2002, bringing the amount of funding nearly back to its original level of $150 million in 1983.

Funding **remained stable** at $140 million until 2005, when there was **a sudden drop** in the space of a year from $140 million to $100 million.

Funding **slowly declined** thereafter, from $100 million in 2006 to $90 million in the final year of 2009.

饼 图

Budgets of Australian and Chinese university students during 2009

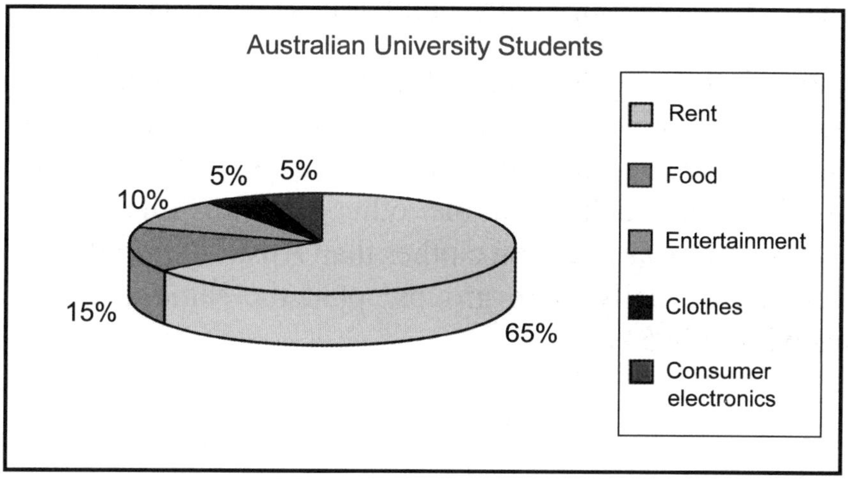

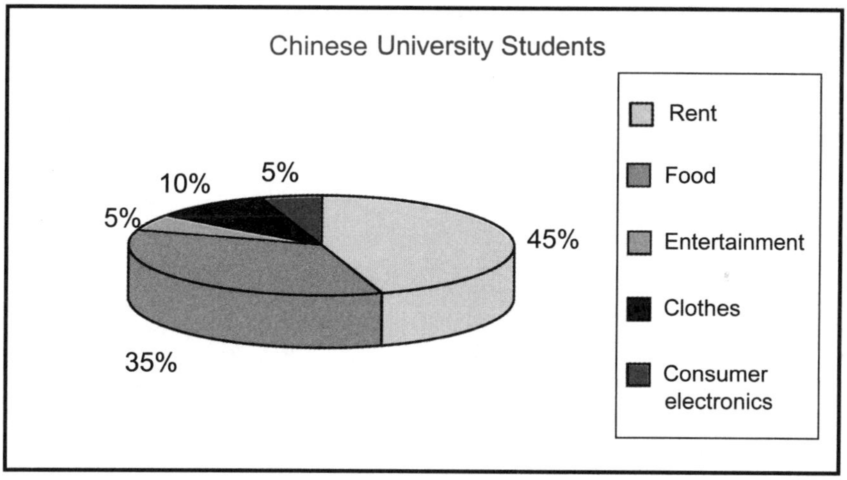

The above set of pie charts compares the budgets and spending patterns of the average Australian university students with that of the average Chinese students during 2009. **As can be seen from** the pie charts, paying rent and buying food were the largest items on students' budgets for both nationalities.

Australian students spent 65% of their budget on rent, **while** Chinese students only spent around two-thirds of this amount. On the other hand, Chinese students spent 35% of their budget on food **in comparison to** Australian students who spent less than a half of this amount. Generally, it appears that rental expenses are **proportionally** higher for Australian students, whereas food expenses are **proportionally** higher for Chinese students.

Spending on clothing, entertainment and consumer electronics all **occupied** smaller **portions** of the budget for both nationalities. Australian students spent 10% of their budget on entertainment **compared to** Chinese students who spent only half as much. On the other hand, Chinese students spent **proportionally** twice as much on clothes than Australian students with 10% and 5% respectively. Finally, both groups spent the same amount on consumer electronics with only 5%.

Bar Chart

条形图

American college students who do each activity at least once a week

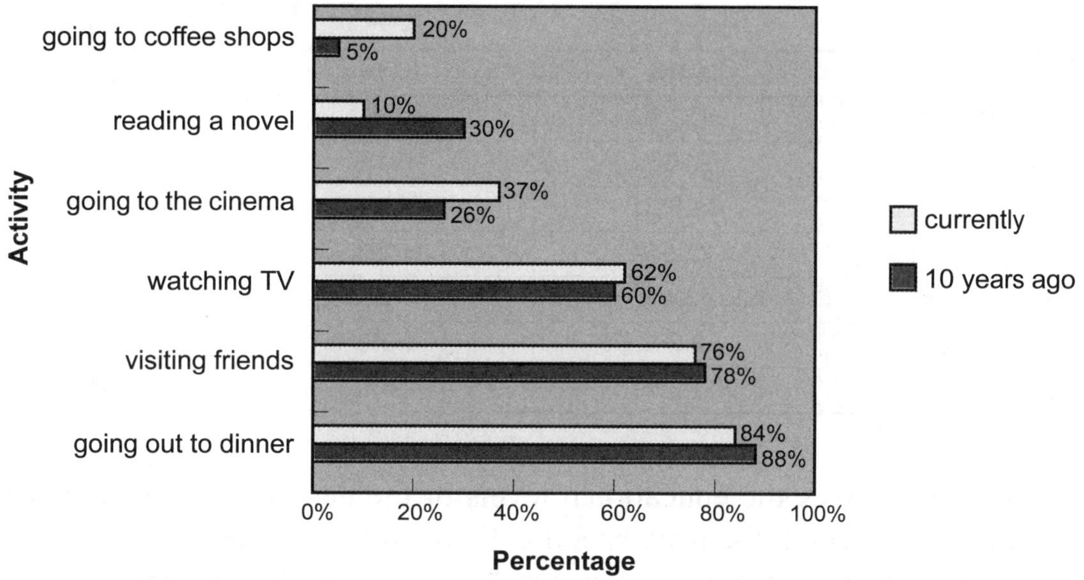

The bar chart **indicates** the leisure-time activities that American college students like to partake in during any given week **compared to** 10 years ago. From the chart it's possible to see that various activities were enjoyed at different levels. However, **minimal change occurred** compared to 10 years ago.

In ascending order, the most popular activities American college students currently enjoy are watching TV (62%), visiting friends (76%) and going out to dinner (84%). These activities are enjoyed to **relatively the same extent** at the same level as 10 years ago, with 60% watching television, 78% visiting friends and 88% going out to dinner at that time.

The most dramatic changes actually occurred within the three activities which were not as popular with American college students on a weekly basis, but are still significant enough to be recorded. For example, ten years ago only 5% of the American college student population went to coffee shops during the week, **in comparison to** now in which the figure has **increased fourfold**. On the other hand, **three times as many** college students read novels ten years ago in comparison to now with 30% and 10% **respectively**. In regards to going to the cinema, around one-third more students watch movies now compared to a decade ago with 37% and 26% respectively.

Table

表格

Level of education of people in India in 2002

	Population	Men	Women
No schooling	9.0%	6.0%	1.2%
Grade school	15.2%	8.7%	21.7%
Junior high school	24.6%	10.1%	39.1%
High school	34.85%	42.3%	27.4%
2 year college	7.85%	15.2%	0.5%
College	13.4%	17.3%	9.5%
Master	2.2%	4.0%	0.4%
PhD	1.0%	1.8%	0.2%

This table **compares** the educational levels of the general adult population in India in the year 2002, focusing specifically on gender differences. **As can be seen from** the table, the figures generally show that the education level of Indian adults who study past high school is quite high with a quarter of the total population of India pursuing tertiary-level study. Having **divided** the population **into** gender, it is clearly evident the difference between males and females is striking.

In a closer analysis of the figures, only **slightly** more than 10% of the Indian female population has received further education beyond high school, **compared with** well over one-third of Indian males. The difference between these figures is even more **drastic** when considering master's or doctoral degrees. 5.8% of the male Indian population has attained one of these degrees, **while** only 0.6% of females did as well as their male counterparts. Finally, it is important to note that over 60% of Indian women have not graduated from high school.

申论写作必备用语

(A) Disagree, Negative, Argue 不同意

These words indicate that your concluding point differs from your previous statement or from what can be generally expected.

nevertheless
nonetheless

虽说如此，不过

My friends all told me that I shouldn't go to Edinburgh to study because it was too far from my home. **Nevertheless**, I went anyway.

not likely
unlikely

不太可能

Considering the public's strong consensus against the war, it is **not likely** that the pro-war candidate will be elected.

on the contrary

相反的

Scientists at Bridge University have recently discovered a medicine that, **on the contrary** to what most people have thought possible, is able to cure a rare liver disease.

it is doubtful that
doubtfully

令人怀疑的

It is doubtful that the legislature will pass the bill because of the strong national opposition to it.

oddly enough
strangely enough

奇怪的是

Oddly enough, the number of Christians in Scotland is much lower than what most people think there are.

on the other hand

另一方面，相反地

On the one hand, studying in an English-speaking country is a very expensive option for many international students and their families. **On the other hand**, the experience and education that these international students receive is invaluable.

in spite of despite

尽管，纵使

In spite of the large amount of scientific progress in the area of AIDS, there are still thousands of people dying of the disease every day.

(B) Agree, Positive, Additional Points 同意及肯定

These words indicate that the writer is in agreement with either a statement said previously by the writer or with a statement said by an outside source. Some of these are also used to point out additional points that agree with the writer's main argument.

naturally

当然

Naturally, the best thing to do when he explodes is to not get angry in return but wait for him to calm down.

undoubtedly

无疑地

This course of action is **undoubtedly** the most profitable to take.

similarly

相同地

Americans tend to enjoy doing adventure sports. **Similarly**, these are also very popular in New Zealand.

in other words/ to put it another way/by that I mean/that is to say

换句话说，也就是说，换个说法就是

Intercultural skills are a valuable asset for employees to have. **In other words**, the more people understand how to interact with each other, the easier it will be to make successful business transactions.

for example
for instance

举例来说

Hong Kong SAR is obsessed with shopping. **For example**, there are even shopping malls in transit stations!

more precisely

说得更明确些

This next election could potentially have a disastrous effect on the opposition party if they don't do well. **More precisely**, if the opposition party only holds 25% of the seats in the legislature, they will need to convince almost half of the members of the ruling party every time they want to pass a new law.

additionally

另外，此外

Global telecommunications have become less expensive over the past few years. **Additionally**, global telecommunication networks have expanded such that they are now able to provide service to many remote areas in the world.

(C) Obviously 显而易见

These phrases indicate that the following statement is of an obvious nature.

it goes without saying that/ everybody knows that/no one can deny that

无庸置疑地，众所皆知地

It goes without saying that if you treat other people well, other people will treat you well.

indeed
certainly

无疑地，的确

Indeed, you will be able to learn Chinese better if you learn it in a Chinese-speaking environment.

obviously

显然，无须怀疑地

Obviously, the best way to study a language is to practise it often.

clearly

清楚地，明白地

He is **clearly** wrong to cheat in exams.

(D) Adding Credibility 增加可信度

In academic writing, your writing gains credibility when you refer to a source other than your own thoughts and opinions. These phrases are used to indicate other sources.

the evidence seems to indicate that

证据似乎显示出

The evidence seems to indicate that the later a couple gets married, the more likely it is that their marriage will last.

people often say that

大家总是说

People often say that if you work hard, you will earn a lot of money, but I think that some of the hardest working people are often the lowest paid, for example nurses or police.

many consider

很多人都认为

Many consider the increasing globalisation of the economy a good thing, but I think that there are serious consequences that are still being ignored.

theoretically

理论上来说

Theoretically, the most advanced life form is humans, but I still think we are capable of doing some of the most inhumane things.

as we all know

正如我们所知

As we all know, technological development has had devastating effects on the earth's environment.

according to

根据

According to the latest advancements in research, stem cells may be used for many medical purposes.

(E) Cause/Effect 原因／结果

In order to develop your opinions in both speaking and writing, it's a good idea to discuss the reasons for and results of certain actions. There are a number of ways to do so. Do not just use because and so.

due to

由于

Due to the damage the typhoon caused, our town has not had clean water for the past four days.

as a consequence
as a result

结果，因此

When I was young, I watched cartoons all the time. **As a consequence**, I became interested in graphic design.

therefore
thereby

因此

English is a very hard language to learn. **Therefore**, it is vital to study hard.

in consequence

结果，后果

It has been raining non-stop for two days. **In consequence**, the rivers are starting to overflow.

thus

因此

Studying at a university can be very expensive. **Thus**, you may want to look for various ways of financing your education.

in order to

为了，使能够

In order to enter most countries legally, you need to have a visa.

(F) Time 时间性

These phrases bring some aspect of time to the sentence.

as time passed

随着时间流逝

As time passed, they became more and more distant to each other.

over the past ... years

在过去的…年间

Over the past ten years, China has become the most important global market.

at present
presently

现在

At present, the world diplomatic community is concerned about the development of democracy in Iraq.

sooner or later
eventually

迟早，终究会

Sooner or later he will realise that the best way to improve his English is to spend more time studying.

previously
beforehand

以前，事前

Previously the only way to communicate was with telephones and fax machines.

simultaneously

同时（进行）地

If we do these two projects **simultaneously**, our staff will be overloaded with work.

in the long run

最终，最后

In the long run, the only way to pay off the deficit is to raise taxes.

during this period
throughout this period

在这段期间

The world has changed a lot in the past century. **During this period** there were two world wars, monumental advances in technology, and great strides in cooperation between countries.

(G) Contrast 对照或否定前后文

The following words introduce that one point is different to another point mentioned.

however

然而

Harvard has one of the best business schools in America, **however**, the tuition is very expensive.

even so

即使如此

The world is becoming more and more of a global community. **Even so**, local culture still plays an important role in people's daily lives.

yet

然而，但是

Your plan sounds good, **yet** I don't think that we can go through with it at this time.

(H) Reinforcing your point, Adding emphasis, Bringing attention to a particular point 强调，引导或强化论述

Adding these phrases brings emphasis to the argument that you are trying to make.

to speak frankly

坦白说

To speak frankly, I didn't have a very good time on my last trip to America.

generally speaking

一般而言

Generally speaking, the best way to make friends from another culture is to become interested in everything about that culture.

by and large

总之

By and large, the best way to succeed in the retail industry is to offer the best quality product at the lowest price.

particularly
in particular

尤其是，特别是

I would suggest reading *Harry Potter*, **particularly** if you enjoy fantasy stories.

at any rate

无论如何

At any rate, the number of people studying English will continue to increase.

as I have said

如我刚刚所说

As I have said, the best place to buy moon cakes is at the bakery down the street.

the point I am making is that

我所强调的重点是

The point I am making is that if we don't get any rest at all, we won't be able to focus well on this project.

considering

顾及，考虑到

Considering the growing popularity of Islamic fundamentalism in Iran, it is likely that its relations with the international community will continue to grow sour.

inevitably

无可避免地

Inevitably, the environment is going to be destroyed by all the pollution we, as a developed society, are producing.

it is important to
it is essential to

重要的是

It is important to remember that the car was invented only a little over a hundred years ago.

it is significant that

极重要的是

It is significant that space-related research and development led to advancements in so many other fields.

I'd like to emphasise

我想强调的是

I'd like to emphasise that I am not condoning abortion. Rather I feel that women should have the right to choose.

I'd like to highlight

我想要强调

I'd like to highlight the point that the professor made about the industrial revolution being the beginning of class warfare.

apart from

除了…之外

Apart from the fact that it is too dark right now, your idea to go to the park would have been a good one.

as well as

除了…之外（但包含此项）

As well as the fact that there is usually a language barrier between people of different countries, there is also often a cultural one.

besides

除…之外（但包含此项），加上

Besides air pollution, noise pollution is also a very serious problem in most large cities.

furthermore

此外，而且

Linguists have been decrying the extinction of local languages for many years. **Furthermore**, if the world continues to globalise at the pace that it has been, there will be even fewer local languages being spoken in the future.

moreover

再者

To be successful at marketing you must understand how people think. **Moreover**, in order to attract people to buy your products, you must understand their hopes and dreams.

in addition

此外

In addition, the widespread use of English means that it is being used for communication between members of non-English speaking countries as well.

what is more

而且

The more information that is shared between people from various cultures, the more we can begin to understand each other. **What is more**, this kind of intercultural communication leads to all of us becoming more tolerant.

(I) Ironic 讽刺

These phrases indicate that the following is ironic, not normal, or unlikely.

ironically

讽刺的是

Ironically, the best way for a country's economy to start growing is for them to have protectionist policies towards its domestic companies and industries.

interestingly

有趣的是

Interestingly, the very economists who most criticise international aid organisations often worked for those same organisations in the past.

it is surprising that

令人惊讶的是

It is surprising that after all of the time I spent working at this company, I only got a raise once.

(J) Order 顺序

* Beginning

firstly
at first

首先

Firstly, I would like to argue that technology makes the world a better place because it helps companies to conduct their business more efficiently.

to begin with

一开始，首先

To begin with, technology makes the world better because it is able to make our lives more convenient.

in the first place

第一

In the first place, technological progress is effective, but only if it proceeds carefully.

* Additional Points

next

次之，其次

Next, we should use more technology in order to help the economy progress.

secondly
thirdly (etc)...

第二，第三…

Secondly, the more we use technology, the less we will be able to think for ourselves.

another point is that

另外一个重点是

Another point is that global communication networks make doing business much more efficient.

* Conclusion or Concluding Points

eventually

最后

Eventually, if technology continues developing, machines will be able to replace human workers.

finally

最后

Finally, we cannot stop technology from becoming more and more sophisticated.

in conclusion
to conclude

结论是

In conclusion, I suggest that the government increase funding directed towards technology-related research and development.

to sum up

总之，概括之

To sum up, I agree with the statement that the government should invest more money into technology-related research and development.

last but not least

（虽然放在最后才说）但最重要的是

Last but not least, in order for countries to cooperate more with each other, they need to have a mutual respect for each other.

the most important point is that

最重要的是

The most important point is that the more we are connected via global information networks, the more we will be able to help each other.

overall

总括而论，总体上

Overall your score was fine; it was only in reading that you did not do so well.

in short
in brief

简言之

In short, the best way to deal with this situation is to keep quiet about it.

(K) 表示顺序（order）的用语及其使用范例

A: Firstly,

The/My first reason is that

To begin with,

B: Secondly,

Next,

Another reason/point is that

My second reason is that

C: Thirdly,

Finally,

My third reason is that

The last reason is that

Last but not least,

D: In short,

In brief,

In other words/By that I mean/That is to say/To put it another way,

E: In conclusion,

To conclude,

To sum up,

Do advances in technology make the world better or worse?

I believe that advances in technology make the world better. The following are three reasons that I have to support my opinion. ____**A**____ technology makes the world better because it helps business people do their business more efficiently. Information technology and computers have made it possible for complicated tasks to be done in much less time than it would have taken without them.

____**B**____ advances in technology allow people to be more connected with each other. The Internet, for example, has allowed businesses and people to communicate with each other much more easily than older methods such as phone, fax or mail.

____**C**____ technology can help us to solve problems, even problems that other technologies created in the first place! On many occasions technology is developed and put into use before people know all of the potential negative side effects. Further research, however, can develop the technology even more so that we can take advantage of its benefits while avoiding its potential shortcomings.

Many people oppose advances in technology because they are both wary of the current level of technology and afraid of potential problems that may be caused by future technologies. However, the most important point to remember is that technology will always be advancing, whether we want it to or not. Therefore, the best way to deal with this situation is to think about ways we can ensure that future advances in technology will not harm our quality of life. ____**D**____ we cannot sacrifice our well-being for future conveniences.

____**E**____ I believe that technological advancement makes the world better! Furthermore, the potential dangers of technological advancement can be prevented by standards and regulations that protect the environment and uphold our morals.

(L) Writing Task 2 写作常用副词、连接词、词组之使用范例

Some people think that a large amount of time and money should be spent on the protection of wild animals and others think it should be spent on the human population. To what extent do you agree or disagree with this opinion?

Humans often forget that we ourselves are an integral part of the larger ecosystem, just as animals are. **However**, unlike animals the influence we wield on the ecosystem has been extremely disproportional to our position as just one species out of many. **Unfortunately**, as the undesignated caretaker of our planet, we tend to also deal with nature out of pure self-interest with barely a care for the other species. **As such**, I would argue that in order for wildlife protection to be sustainably feasible, it must offer benefits for humans. It is **also** my position that it definitely does offer many advantages for humans as both the human population and animal population are interdependent to the extent that to maintain the current status of animal protection would be tantamount to signing our own death warrant. **Hence**, spending needed money on wildlife protection would be equivalent to spending money on the human population, killing two birds with one stone, **so to speak**.

What exactly are the benefits of protecting wild animals? **First**, protection of animals often involves setting aside nature preserves which can and do serve as the lungs of our earth, counterbalancing the harmful pollution humans produce. **Second**, such preserves offer us the opportunity to get in touch with nature again through strolls, hikes and other activities, providing mental relief from the stress of urban civilisation. **In addition**, these natural habitats serve as places where children can learn about life through the flora and fauna. **Furthermore**, as is often touted in the case of preserving the Amazon basin, the animals themselves along with the rich variety of plant life might provide untold sources for possible miracle drugs to cure the major diseases now afflicting humankind **such as** cancer, AIDS, etc. These islands of greenery also act as research sites for studying animal and plant life, shedding light upon biology, botany, and human life itself. And **last but not least**, preserving wildlife will give many of us a guiltless conscience, **knowing that** we did not selfishly exterminate other life forms and left them for future generations to enjoy and study. We can show ourselves and our descendants that we consider life, **whether** human **or** animal, to be sacred and prove to ourselves that humanity still has some compassion.

In conclusion, when discussed from the vantage point of the self-serving needs of humans, the argument for the protection of wild animals will be sufficiently persuasive to ensure that some wildlife forms will survive. But I am not so naive as to believe that vast tracts of land along with a menagerie of wildlife forms will be preserved in great numbers because humans will inevitably continue to encroach upon the habitat of wild animals out of self-interest. **In the end**, **however**, while animals may pay the ultimate price of extinction, our interdependence on this very same environment will cause us to follow in their wake. But unlike the innocent wild animals we will exit this world with a guilty conscience, and our utterly selfish acts against nature will have **ironically** caused us to lose our very own humanity.

Index

索引

A

B

C

D

I

J

K

L

M

N

O

P

S

T

U

V